THE CAREER SUCCESS FORMULA

PROVEN CAREER DEVELOPMENT ADVICE AND FINDING REWARDING EMPLOYMENT FOR YOUNG ADULTS AND COLLEGE GRADUATES

BUKKY EKINE-OGUNLANA

TCECPUBLISHING.COM

© Copyright Bukky Ekine-Ogunlana 2021 – All rights reserved.

The content contained within this book may not be reproduced, duplicated or transmitted without direct written permission from the author or the publisher.

Under no circumstance will any blame or legal responsibility be held against the publisher, or author, for any damages, reparation, or monetary loss due to the information contained within this book. Either directly or indirectly. You are responsible for your own choices, actions and results.

Legal Notice:

This book is copyright protected. This book is only for personal use. You cannot amend, distribute, sell, use, quote or paraphrase any part, or the content within this book, without the author or publisher's consent.

Disclaimer Notice:

Please note the information contained within this document is for educational and entertainment purposes only. All effort has been executed to present accurate, up-to-date, and reliable, complete information. No warranties of any kind are declared or implied. Readers acknowledge that the author is not engaging in the rendering of legal, financial, medical or professional advice. The content within this book has been derived from various sources. Please consult a licensed professional before attempting any techniques outlined in this book

By reading this book, the reader agrees that under no circumstances is the author responsible for any losses, direct or indirect, which are incurred as a result of the use of the information contained within this document, including, but not limited to,—errors, omissions, or inaccuracies.

Published by

TCEC Publishing

TCEC House

14-18 Ada Street, London Fields,

E8 4QU, England, Great Britain.

CONTENTS

Introduction	9
1. How to Make a Career Choice	23
2. Building A Career	39
3. Women and Careers	52
4. Career Advice for Graduates: What Should I Be?	93
5. Career Management	115
6. Career Killer	123
Conclusion	145
Other Books You'll Love!	147
References	149

DEDICATION

This lovely book is dedicated to all the beautiful students all over the world who, over the years, have passed through the T.C.E.C young adult's program. Thanks for the opportunity to serve you and invest in your colorful and bright future.

Your free gift!

Voucher ID: NGH0001

As a way of saying thank you for purchasing this book, I am offering you a free gift at the end of the book

INTRODUCTION

Are you looking for a potential career fresh out of university? Are you a professional looking to switch to a different career stream? Or perhaps you are a young adult on the hunt for the perfect job. If you fall into any of these categories or can relate to any of these scenarios in some capacity, then this book is right for you.

Finding a career that suits your interests, passions, needs, and lifestyle can be a very daunting task, specifically if you are fresh out of school. With this book, you will understand what makes a career, why it can sometimes be frustrating when you do not get the job you want, and what you can do to land a promising career as a fresh graduate young adult.

We generally define a career as a person's job during their working life. This definition is broad and includes changes such as the acquisition of skills and qualifications.

Usually, however, we associate a lot more with a career than that, namely advancement, not only in the hierarchy of a company but also socially. That means a higher position, more salary, a better company car, a more excellent office, etc. When we talk about someone who has made a career, we often imagine an absolute high-flyer with the best degrees, a quick promotion, and a résumé with whom international head-hunters would strike immediately.

The career is an individual's metaphorical "journey" through learning, work and other aspects of life. There are several ways to define a career, and the term is used in various ways. It is an omnipresent topic, not only in our career bible but in school, during studies, or in everyday life: careers are planned, discussed, and highlighted everywhere. Everyone wants to have a career, be successful, and achieve something. Few, however, think about what that means: making a career. The way is not prescribed; it does not always have to go up steeply.

Much more importantly: a career is what you make of it and what you expect from it. We show what makes a career and what possibilities there are to shape your career.

Finding a career that suits you and fulfills all of your needs may take some trial and error, which instills fear in many people because of the uncertainty that lies ahead. While it can be a stress-inducing situation, it is essential to overcome the negative outlook you may have on this journey and develop an attitude that seeks to fulfill yourself and your future truly.

This is better clearly said than done, but an excellent way to look at this is by approaching your career with creativity in mind. It is essential to think about your work's impact and its effect on those around you. This approach of coloring outside the lines, rather than falling into the structure and rules that limit you in the workplace, often yields better results. People are less afraid to take risks and truly challenge themselves in the workplace. This can mean taking on more tasks or responsibilities, branching out into other areas of interest, or even merely reaching out to those around them and being more outspoken in social situations. This differs from one person to another person and is based on their job and what it entails. But that is not to say that creativity will carry you to new heights if you keep it in mind with every task you do.

The underlying idea behind being creative with your career lies in this Jewish phenomenon: "With your certificate, you must learn another trade." Humans are multifaceted and capable of accomplishing so much more than we might think and anticipate. The circumstances that affect our lives can hit us when we are least expecting it, thus changing the course of our lives dramatically, career included. Because you can be displaced at any time, the important thing is to continually evolve and challenge yourself to acquire more skills so that you can carve a career path that truly fits you and what fascinates you, no matter what variables shape your life. The mantra is to "always be a student" because there will always be new skills to be mastered and learn. This mindset prepares you for the unknown and often spurs on burgeoning entrepreneurial spirits that most people do not realize they have.

I once discussed this with a friend of mine who was a lawyer. He had experienced a dramatic shift in life that inspired some of the basis for this book. He said the words: "These hands have provided for my necessities," which were tremendously profound and inspiring. He had attended an Ivy League law school and worked at a top law firm in Chicago. Despite having an incredibly successful career by most standards, he no longer went to court as a lawyer because he found that it was no longer a fulfilling job. What was once a role that fueled his passions for helping people become a high-strung environment that valued monetary gain above all else. Disillusioned, he ended up quitting and finding success in making tents, a newly acquired hobby that found him tapping into an entrepreneurial spirit he never knew he had.

While his career change was dramatic and certainly drastic for many, the vital thing to note here is that he did not feel limited at any point because he was always bearing the idea of a higher purpose. While giving up his law career was a huge step, he found fulfillment by staying true to his talents of helping others. He understood that burying his talents deprived others of his creations.

As the world's populace continues to grow and shows no signs of slowing down, more jobs are being cut. With technology replacing a good portion of the working sector every year, an individual's career prospects continue to diminish. The future is looking increasingly bleak for job seekers, which leaves plenty of room for job creators, entrepreneurs, and the likes of people who use their skills to make products and services that serve society. But the challenge lies in carving out a niche. How does one even begin to find a need and create a sustainable job and provide a living? One of the best strategies to do so is to expose yourself to knowledge every day and find new skills to grasp the services and products that the world does not know it needs.

Everyone is familiar with career, but hardly anyone knows where the word comes from. The term comes from the French carrière, which means something like racing track or career. Precisely what characterizes what we mean by today's career: We are in the race, are in constant competition, must give 120 percent, the others depend upon. Higher, faster, further and more successful.

A professional career can be designed and realized in many ways. Often only financial factors are taken into account to assess how successful the occupation is. However, that alone is not enough and ignores other factors such as personal satisfaction and fulfillment.

To make the diversity of the career clearer to you, this book will show you various careers and opportunities:

LEADERSHIP CAREER

This form describes what is classically understood as making a career. You work your way up in a company, climb the career ladder step by step, become a leader and take on significant responsibility. For teams, for projects, for entire companies, when you become a top manager. In a management career, a career means a position at the top, very high pay, and social advancement, which relates to the professional.

PROFESSIONAL CAREER

A professional career is not necessarily about hierarchical advancement in the profession but about becoming an expert in your field. So, you do not strive for managerial responsibility but steadily develop your qualifications, acquire in-depth know-how and have a knowledge advantage over other employees and competitors. In this way, you will become a sought-after and valuable expert highly valued by employers and negotiate a fair salary accordingly.

INDEPENDENCE

You can make a career not only with an employer but also with your own company. In self-employment, you can set up your own business, implement an idea or make a dream come true. At the same time, you become your boss, but you also bear a greater risk. Many people appreciate the greater freedom in a self-employed career because you are not bound by strict guidelines and instructions from the boss. Instead, you can make your own decisions.

FREELANCER

As a freelancer, you offer your services and skills to companies and other clients. You also enjoy greater freedom because a company does not directly employ you. On the other hand, you always must receive new orders; otherwise, no payments will be accepted. Besides, freelancers are not active and in demand in all industries.

PROJECT CAREER

The so-called project career lies somewhere between a freelancer and a specialist career. With your extensive knowledge in a specific area, you will work on projects and sometimes even lead them, but an employer or client will only employ you for the project's duration.

EMPLOYEE

In this context, one often finds the phrase: someone is only an employee. This shows the wrong view because even an employee can have a successful and promising career according to their imagination. Not everyone focuses on their job in life; some want a better work-life balance and do not want to work overtime every day to advance. As an employee in a position that makes you happy, you have exactly the career that suits you.

THE GOAL IN MIND

However, one essential aspect seems to be missing from this general definition. After all, what if you have not got where you wanted to go professionally? Those who do not exhaust their potential remain completely below their possibilities, find their tasks boring, and are permanently dissatisfied, sooner or later lose their motivation to work and identify with their job. Such a person is unlikely to claim to have made a career.

Career expert and founder of the office for career strategy, Jürgen Hesse, says: "In our daily advice, we repeatedly experience that the delighted employees are those who have achieved their project. I would make a career describe as a state of affairs that, looking back, clarifies that I have already successfully taken this professional development. Here I am and see a worthwhile, professional goal right in front of my eyes, which I will certainly achieve very soon." So, it is about a professional goal you have set yourself. And that can turn out very differently - whether you want to become a gardener, space researcher, department head, or independent management consultant. The two crucial questions are always: What is your goal, and how do you get there?

Those who can no longer put their personal goals into practice need to compare themselves with others and their professional life courses. However, some people do not even know exactly what their future careers should look like. So what? After all, you can only follow your path if you know where it should lead you. So, first find out what you want and above all think about your competencies, your talents, abilities and skills, your professional and personal interests and inclinations.

A seminar on potential analysis can help you to get on track with yourself and your wishes. With this changed perspective on careers, Angela Sommer suddenly finds it very easy to look forward to her class reunion. Because she has achieved exactly what she always wanted - she does exactly the job that she enjoys and gives her time to her family. So, if a former classmate asks her: "What are you doing?" She will answer very simply and confidently: "I've made a career."

RETHINKING CAREER

But change is slowly taking place. In the prior, it was frowned upon and associated with the weakness to take a break. You can now find "sabbaticals" or parental leave very often listed in the résumés. Fathers take time off to have time for their families, and young people are increasingly taking sabbaticals to travel the world or to rethink their previous lives.

In the meantime, many companies, especially agile organizations, see this as positive. We are not looking for perfect employees, but team members who find creative solutions with whom we enjoy working with and strive for the next highest position and meaning. An experience that is acquired outside of traditional career paths, such as a trip around the world, is essential for companies that encourage "out of the box" thinking.

People often take one more step in the Anglo-Saxon world: so-called "zigzag" CVs are not uncommon but regular. While (supposedly) secure jobs and careers are still upheld in Germany, Americans, for example, look around much more often for new jobs and sometimes go more unconventional ways than we are used to in the country. Of course, financial aspects are in the foreground due to the low coverage and personal development level. While it is complicated to switch to controlling in Germany after years of marketing experience, this is not uncommon in other countries. Or it is normal to have worked as a barista in the meantime.

INDIVIDUAL CAREER PATHS AND DEVELOPMENT OPPORTUNITIES

This is nice because you may only discover unrecognized talents or potentials once you have tried something different. Or it confirms that the current job is precisely right for you. For me, a career is much more than climbing a ladder (and that usually leads to the top), but rather a development. A development process in which you recognize strengths, develop talents, and thus assemble your career path.

I am a certified career coach myself. Working with Young Adults, but I am not 100% happy with this. Because even during the apprenticeship, there were so many topics that you might not associate with the title. It was much more about development areas, how these can be addressed, identified, and then implemented in the job. How to recognize and achieve goals, arrive on the job market, but not with yourself.

Classic careers will continue to exist, just like people who have detailed résumés and are treated as "aspiring employees" or "high potentials." And that is just as well! Such people naturally have entirely different issues when they turn to me than at a crossroads. But they too have careers, but the definition may be different, and so are the topics in the coaching process.

After reading this book, please feel free to leave a review based on your findings and how useful the book was to you. I would be incredibly thankful if you could take 60 seconds to write a brief review on the platform of purchase, even if it's just a few sentences!

HOW TO MAKE A CAREER CHOICE

People mostly have problems based on their career planning strategies and choice making. Knowledge base comes from knowing what job is right for you and test to see what career is best for you.

Today we face an incredible number of opportunities to develop professionally. That is wonderful. It offers a chance to live out our various talents. At the same time, it also raises the pressure to find an area, an industry, an activity that fulfills us, if possible, until the end of our (professional) life and in that case "to make a career," that is, to advance us.

My opinion: We no longer need to submit to this pressure today. We can actively and independently shape what a career is for us and how we want to shape it. More in the sense of a trade which is winding and with a depth that we have designed for ourselves. If you have that, then go for it.

With thousands of opportunities, how will you choose a career that is right for you? If you do not know what you want to do, the task may seem impossible. Fortunately, it is not. Follow organized proceedings, and you will increase your chances of making the right decision.

Plenty of people have graduated from college and entered the workforce to find out that their skillset and interests would be better suited in a different field that requires additional schooling. Going back to college at the non-typical college age is perfectly acceptable. It is, in fact, commendable because it shows that you are frequently willing to challenge yourself and evolve as an individual to find your niche and promote your efforts in a field that would better suit it.

So, take note of this in your mind that if you are a young adult struggling to find where you might thrive. The world is your oyster, and the privileges seem limitless because they are. There are so many opportunities out there if you truly take your time to research and educate yourself on the prospects that lie ahead of you. Remember that your decision at eighteen years old does not define the trajectory of the rest of your life. Career changes are regular and part of life. Ultimately, you have to prioritize yourself and put your needs above societal expectations.

ASSESS YOURSELF

Before you can choose the right profession, you must learn about yourself. Your values, interests, soft skills, and aptitudes, combined with your makeup or personality type, make some occupations a good fit for you and others completely inappropriate. While you are still in university, always look up job prospects. You need to check yourself on what you want. The goal is to take a deep dive into yourself to consider everything that has struck a chord with you in your life to go about deciding if this is something you want to pursue when you age. This is also the perfect time to try out internships or part-time jobs. While many of these positions might be unpaid, the experience you receive in return is precious and can help you figure out where you might want to focus your efforts.

Use self-assessment tools and trade tests to gather information about your traits and, subsequently, generate a list of lines of works that are the best fit based on them. Some individuals choose to work with a career counselor or other career development professionals who can help them navigate this process.

For some people, figuring out their career path is a no-brainer. School years can facilitate strengths like mathematics and science that lead to career paths in technology or medicine. For others, the answer is not so simple and might take ample trial and error to find the best fit for them. Whichever route you have taken, remember that there is no wrong answer.

MAKE A LIST OF OCCUPATIONS TO EXPLORE

You possibly have multiple lists of lines of works in front of you at this point—one generated by any of the self-assessment tools or mechanism you used. To keep yourself organized, you shall combine them into one master list.

First, look for careers that show on multiple lists and copy them onto a blank page. Title or label it "Occupations to Explore." Your self-assessments indicated they are an acceptable fit for you based on several of your traits, so they are worth exploring.

Next, find occupations or work on your lists that appeal to you. They can be careers you know a bit about and want to explore further. Also, include professions about which you do not know much. You might learn something unexpected.

EXPLORE THE OCCUPATIONS ON YOUR LIST

At this point, you will be thrilled you managed to narrow your list down to only 10 to 20 options. Now you can get some necessary information about each of the occupations on your list.

Find job descriptions, educational training, and licensing requirements in published sources. Learn about leading opportunities. Use government-produced labor market knowledge to get data about earnings and job outlook.

CREATE A "SHORT LIST"

Now you have more knowledge, start to narrow down your list table even further. Based on what you studied from your investigation so far, begin eliminating the careers you do not want to pursue any further. You will end up with two to five lines of works or crafts on your "shortlist."

If your reasons for finding a line of work unacceptable are non-negotiable, cross it off your list. Eliminate everything with duties that do not appeal to you. Eliminate professions that have weak job outlooks. Get rid of any line of work if you are unable or unwilling to fulfill the educational or other requirements or if you lack some of the soft skills necessary to succeed in it.

Shortlisting careers is essential to not end up with a job that makes you feel constant frustration and regret later.

Take the time to research and put effort into considering the careers that interest you. While it is not permanent, it will be a substantial commitment to finally decide on the trades that pique your interest.

CONDUCT INFORMATIONAL INTERVIEWS

When you have only a few occupations or works left on your list, begin doing a more in-depth analysis. Arrange a meet-up with people who work in the professions in which you are interested. They can provide firsthand knowledge about the job on your shortlist. Access your network, including LinkedIn, to find individuals with whom to have these informational interviews.

You can also check out job reviews on these careers online or ask others what they think. It is good to have input from other people, especially those working in these careers. This will help you get an idea of what to expect from them. You can also approach your professors or mentors in university to gauge their inputs on these careers.

This is also the gateway to networking. This helps develop some lasting relationships that can help your career trajectory later on in life, whether you seek to advance your career or completely take a different pathway. In-depth research and making connections with like-minded people can broaden the horizon and expose you to jobs you might have never considered.

Furthermore, networking from a young age prepares you later on in your career, when you have to face more seniors and executives. Having the experience can set you apart from coworkers and competition because you are seasoned and well-prepared with the expertise needed to meet these high-intensity situations.

MAKE YOUR CAREER CHOICE

Lastly, after doing all your research, you are probably ready to make your choice. Pick the occupation you think will bring you the most satisfaction based on all the information you have gathered. Realize that you are allowed to do-overs if you change your mind about your choice at any point in your life. A lot of people change their careers at least a few times.

Remember that this is just your initial career. Do not expect that this will be your only career in life unless you want it to be. You can change jobs as much as you want in the future. But that does not also mean that you slack off. You still have to do your best once you start working.

IDENTIFY YOUR GOALS

Once you make a choice, identify your long- and short-term goals. This will help to chart a course toward eventually landing work in your decided field. Long-term objectives typically take about three to five years to reach, while you can usually fulfill a short-term purpose in six months to about three years.

Let the research you did about required schooling, education, and training be your guide. If you do not have all the specifics, do some more research. Once you have all the data you need, set your goals. An example of a long-term objective would be completing your schooling and training. Short-term objectives include applying to college, apprenticeships, other training programs, and internships.

Having more significant, overarching goals can help you home in on the finer details that are often more difficult to iron out. Bigger goals help define the direction you want to go in because it is the first step needed to figure out important details like your major in college or an internship you might find worthwhile pursuing.

WRITE A CAREER ACTION PLAN

Put together a progressive career action plan, a written document that lays out all the steps or tracks you will have to take to reach your objectives. Visualize it as a road map that can take you from point A to B, then to C and D. Pen down all your short- and long-term objectives and the steps you will have to take to reach each one. Add any anticipated barriers that could get in the way of achieving your dreams—and the ways you can overcome them.

MEET WITH AN ADVISOR

If you are in school, this is the perfect time to take advantage of all of the career advisors and counselors that are specifically put in place to help you figure out your needs. Even without a solid plan, career advisors can help you develop a plan to put into motion. This way, if you are in school and trying to figure out what to major in, you will fulfill all of the prerequisites required to give yourself options when the time comes to make a final decision on what exactly you intend to pursue.

Use the resources available

Take advantage of your school's events that get you connected with industry professionals who have experience with recruiting and internships. Getting advice directly from the source is tremendously valuable and can offer insight into whether this career path you have chosen is the best fit for you. It is essential to ask the right questions and get the most transparent and honest answers, and these advisors are here specifically to do so.

Despite your research and networking efforts, you might find that deciding on a career that fits all of your interests is very difficult. Many students face this and leave their majors undeclared until the last minute. When graduation arrives, these young adults panic and make last-minute decisions on their careers that they later regret. You may not believe me, but this too is par for the course.

For some, this might indicate that you may have to carve out your niche to create a career that truly suits your interests, goals, and ambitions in life. Gaining new skills and experience is the way to do this. Perhaps you still need foundational knowledge in a broad subject like a business to tap into your entrepreneurial side. Or maybe interning in areas that interest you can help you draw inspiration for your own business.

And for many others, this might be a sign that having real-life experience will indeed give the final push into a particular direction to make a more well-informed decision. Many young adults choose to intern and work in various positions as soon as they graduate to explore career options in a more hands-on way.

This may sound like it is a lot of work—and it is. But it is a lot easier to forge a career route when you know what you wish. Taking these steps initially will save you many trials, struggles, and uncertainty in the long run.

HOW TO KNOW IF YOU'VE CHOSEN THE WRONG CAREER

There are quite a minority of tell-tale signs that indicate if the career path you are in is not the right one for you. Many people can tell as soon as they step foot into their workplace on the first day and observe other team members' dynamics. But quitting a job can be tremendously intimidating because it brings uncertainty and anxiety about finding your next one, and many people choose to stick it out because they simply do not have the luxury to quit. Bills have to be paid, and making a living is more important than finding fulfillment, right?

Wrong. Compromising yourself, your beliefs, and your values for a job can be extremely draining for an individual. Going to work every day with people you do not like can be extremely demotivating and demoralizing. These factors have an immense impact on your quality of life and can take a significant toll on your mental health and stability. If you find that you are faced with these feelings, it might be time to begin the transition process in your job, perhaps to a different department, role, or altogether a different route.

Indicators that it might be such a time to quit your job:

- Your work is not challenging nor fulfilling. Instead, you find yourself feeling drained every time, and you have a negative outlook on your work, regardless of how well you have executed it. This negative outlook can manifest into a mindset that affects your entire day and drags you down.

- Your strengths are never utilized. Completing your work is a constant uphill battle, and you find yourself not being able to take advantage of your unique skillset in your professional life.
- You are too comfortable in your position. While most people aspire for comfort and having confidence when it comes to their jobs, you can have too much of a good thing. If you find that you are not being challenged in any way, this might be the time to move onto something with higher stakes. Being able to push yourself to learn and grow is one of the most critical parts of a career.
- Lack of promotions. Sometimes being too comfortable in your position indicates that it is time to move onto a more prominent role. But suppose your company does not support growth or facilitate your experience by giving you more responsibilities. This can lead to a sense of stagnation that makes you feel restless and dissatisfied.
- You have given your job 110%. You cannot possibly dedicate any more time or energy,

given that you are one individual trying to ensure the best results every time. Yet, you find that you are unfulfilled, and your results are never as good as you would like. This could indicate that this career you have chosen is not a good fit for you, and it might be time to move onto something different.

- You find yourself unsatisfied with the industry. Perhaps it is the unruly behavior that is allowed, like workplace harassment or discrimination. Or maybe it is a work culture that has been normalized, where it is toxic and extremely harmful for your mental health. This is a massive sign that the industry does not align with your personal beliefs, and you need to move on to something else.
- You are bringing home the negativity. It is one thing to have a bad day at work. But once you start bridging that same negative mindset into your household, you begin to affect those around you inadvertently.
- You feel suffocated. This can be the case for many creatives who do not realize that their passions lie in them thinking outside of the

box rather than subscribing to another corporate cog.
- Continually thinking about quitting might be a more significant sign than you think. Take time to seriously consider why you are always contemplating quitting your job and weighing the pros and cons.

BUILDING A CAREER

Careers do not fall from the sky. Even with a little bit of hard work and perseverance, the journey is far from over. Is the next or later step on the career ladder long overdue? Then it is time to take your career development into your own hands. Here are eight tips for your professional advancement.

"Building a career" means more than a raise in salary

Behind the concept of professional success, there are very different definitions and understandings of career. However, this refers to the professional career in general, which includes aspects of salary, the classic "ascending" hierarchies in a company, and the assumption of responsibility. However, a digital market survey and opinion research survey show more to a career than money and power—more than 75% name the aspect of professional freedom as a distinguishing feature of a successful career. Space of decision and flexible working hours, and an excellent work-life balance are part of a successful - and healthy - career. The enjoyment of the job, the individual self-realization, and the personal level of awareness in the own branch are ranked higher than the status of the salary and the company hierarchy's rank.

I used to think that making a career means finding a clear path, very determined, and quickly. Today I define "career" very differently.

"CAREER" MEANS HAVING CONSTANT PRESSURE

I put myself under pressure for a long time. It was so important to me to have a career that shines and sparkles on the outside. With which I can impress and which my family can proudly talk about. Today, I could let go of this claim and follow my vision of an authentic career. I ask myself the following questions:

What does it mean to have a trade? And what should your job look like?

And I am sure that young adults like you also have these expectations and are asking the same questions. Today I am at a point where I know: work is part of my life, and at the same time, work is not my life. Just a few years ago, I found it hard to imagine finding recognition and acceptance when I am not productive, cannot show significant results, and when I am just there.

I still love creating things and being successful, but for different reasons. It used to be elementary for me to have a job that makes my family proud and calms them down and is therefore associated with a good salary (my fallacy: a lot of money = a lot of recognition = more excellent personal value). From today's perspective, of course, my choice of profession for finance can also be questioned in terms of acceptance and recognition, but ten years ago, it promised a successful career. And that is what I wanted, right?

WHAT MAKES SUCCESSFUL PEOPLE?

Varied factors and character traits can facilitate a career boost. In particular, people with a very self-confident demeanor, the right specialist knowledge, a strong passion for the industry, and a thriving network, have the best starting career opportunities. But that character traits and soft skills will help you achieve happiness in your career? In general, however, the study of market and opinion research identified the following characteristics and traits as career pushes:

- Communication skills
- Resilience
- Professional competence
- Power of decision
- Self-confidence
- Determination
- Conflict resolution skills
- Sense of responsibility
- Reliability

The characteristics that appear further down in the ranking that should not be underestimated include social skills: teamwork and critical skills, empathy or integrity, and honesty. Nevertheless, a certain amount of self-marketing and self-staging is required in most industries and positions for a career kick, which gives some people a significant advantage by their nature - regardless of talent.

WHAT DOES IT MEAN TO HAVE A SUCCESSFUL CAREER?

The term career is completely unspectacular on its own and is defined as follows (see Wikipedia):

1. A person's career is his professional life, sober and unbiased
2. Every operational sequence of positions of a person in a functional structure, technical and value-free.

WHAT IS A RELAXED DEFINITION OF CAREER?

I like to see a career as a person's career in their professional life and view it more neutrally. This leaves the space open for many creative options for personal career decisions. Because while when you think of a career, you often think of an ascending staircase, a career path can be winding, branching off, going up and down, turning a loop, just like (professional) life.

The supposed ideal career: school, studies/training that are fun, a job that suits me well and is fulfilling, advancement in this job that suits me so well, money, influence, leadership, is only granted to a few. Lucky guys?

CAN A CAREER ALSO BE CALLED A CAREER?

Decide for yourself. Whether you are still in university, a fresh graduate, or a young adult on their first leg of job search, you need to ask these questions:

- Can your career have a career character?
- Is it okay if you have studied business administration and discover that your heartbeat is for social education?
- Do you want to attempt a different branch of your company?
- Can you start another degree? Can you create your own business?
- Can you switch back to a permanent position from self-employment?

I have grappled with similar questions about my career. And it was good to give permission finally to myself: Yes, I can. I can try things out, and I can make new turns and follow them. And if I get to a dead-end, I can turn around and take another turn—none of this changes anything about my worth. I only win—experience, knowledge, and contacts. It would be best if you did the same.

COURAGE PAYS OFF

Asking yourself these questions takes courage and perseverance. Changing your choices before you grab onto a specific career takes time. You will have to prepare things, make contacts, write applications, and face setbacks. Your acquaintances, friends, and family will question your decisions, mostly because they want to protect you (and maybe themselves) and because they mean well with you.

8 TIPS FOR A CAREER

Anyone who has wished to pursue a career for a long time and has stagnated may have been in the same job at the same company for some time—the same thing with fresh graduates. You may have thought of your ideal career for so long that you end up missing out on other opportunities because you are settled with your "ideal" job.

Do not forget that good chances of a higher career level have people whose professional context is changing - such as when a job changes. Ideally, you will go through an average of three to four job changes up to your career's peak to gain different professional experience and still not lose a sure consistency in your job. With these eight tips for starting a career, your professional happiness comes one step closer:

Importance of career: First, make yourself aware that professional advancement is for you personally. One is often strongly influenced by social ideals and career paths customary in the industry and thereby loses sight of individual career happiness.

1. **Goodbye perfectionism**: If you set yourself too high a standard, you will never meet your criteria. The pursuit of perfection instantly ends in frustration and demotivation. Recognize your strengths but also your learning areas and stay successful in this way.
2. **Mistakes = valuable experience**: The schooling fields also include reflecting on small and large errors. The aim here is to

understand that mistakes are valuable enrichment for you. This is the only way to make progress in terms of soft and hard skills. That means gaining experience - no matter what! Your self-presentation and rhetorical skills do not necessarily work naturally as a career starter. Here, you need to learn from your mistakes and get the best out of your talent. This will eventually help you as you search for the right job.

3. **Flexible strategies**: Many ways lead to the goal. Do not stick to a single path to your dream job; keep several options open - including a possible career as a career change. Define areas and strategies and use them flexibly, depending on the situation and company. Those who remain flexible in their requirements also have better cards in salary and job negotiations.

4. **Defeat habits**: Everyone has "bad habits" that make it difficult for themselves or others somehow. Postponing annoying tasks, regularly arriving late at meetings, being unreliable in keeping promises, etc., should never be cultivated. The first step is when you look at your bad habits. Do not let them

get in your way. Discard old habits through self-discipline.

5. **Initiate and do not wait**: You must act to achieve your goals. Do not wait until you are offered a career opportunity. Take the initiative yourself - for example, an internship change abroad. If you wish to make a career, you must take responsibility for yourself. Individuals who act independently focus on opportunities and do not worry about guilt when something does not go according to plan. Careerists ask themselves: what could I have done differently or better? Take on the problem and refrain from justifying yourself. Regular Staff meetings with your supervisor will also help towards your career.

6. **Invest in networks**: You climb the career ladder step by step. You can also observe this when other role models and careers inspire you in similar industries. Research possible contact points with people who share your interests: Lectures, conferences, and trade fairs are excellent opportunities to get to know people in a small group. Caution: Don't network just for the sake of networking! A

sizeable online network on Xing or LinkedIn is by no means a guarantee of success. Quality before quantity!
7. **"No" to the decision dilemma**: People who put decisions on the back burner and let themselves be drifted lose respect both for others and for themselves. Some people do not want to decide out of uncertainty. Of course, this means that the decision will be made for you by someone else. Again and again, critics and pessimists will cross your career path. Do not let their negative attitudes infect you. Believe in yourself and your abilities!

The pressure to have a successful career is a real and tangible aspect of entering the workforce. The pressure to grind and get into the nitty-gritty of working to succeed is continuously being forced onto young adults because this is the work culture that we have established as the norm. But "success" in itself can mean a lot of different things for many other people. For some, success looks like a certain amount of money in their bank account. Some view success as being able to own a house. At the same time, some see success as a state of mind rather than material goods, where success is peace of mind from worries.

One thing is exact, "success" varies from person to person. When it comes down to the real it, it is up to you to decide what you want to amount to in your lifetime. Societal pressures will continue to exist and challenge you down to your core but stay true to your ambitions and goals.

This was abundantly clear when I had a conversation with a young entrepreneur who had just graduated from college. At the age of twenty- four, he had sold off his first tech company in a seven-figure deal. He was set for life. Yet upon speaking to him, it was evident that the money was not his primary concern like it would have been for most young adults of his age. Instead, he was already developing his next piece of technology that he hoped would be implemented in schools all across the country. He was incredibly transparent when he shared that the money was exciting at first. Still, the real excitement lay that now he could fund his passions, making educational teaching accessible and affordable. Aside from being a noble and impressive pursuit, it was astounding to me that this 24-year-old was not planning on blowing through his money by buying luxury cars and gadgets.

The fact is that while money seems to keep the world spinning, it cannot possibly begin to fill deep emotional voids like passion.

WOMEN AND CAREERS

Career opportunities for women have continued to improve in recent years. Nevertheless, young female professionals "to achieve anything" do not always match gender-specific professional realities. For women to advance professionally, not only the professional qualifications but especially the career-enhancing character traits must be right. Family planning can also become a significant obstacle to a career as a woman. Even if you are on maternity leave, it does not necessarily have to lead to the end of career advancement. The differences between the sexes affect women's natural reproductive role and differences in terms of care obligations after childbirth, part-time work, and income. The female employment rate in Austria has been increasing for years, with the number of women fully employed tending to stagnate. The difference in wages or salaries between women and men (gender pay gap) in Austria remains a significant career problem for women with a difference of 20% (2016) - well above the average EU gap of 16.2%.

The good news first: there have never been so many well-educated women as there are today. In terms of education, women are ahead by a nose. The proportion of women graduating from university is currently 56% in Austria and 79% in teacher training colleges.

And yet data from Statistics in Austria shows: Even if they are better educated, women still earn less than men, work more than before, and more often sit in less lucrative

Part-time positions. The sad reality is that women and men doing the same job are not playing the field.

The fact is that women often face an uphill battle, especially in specific industries that males heavily dominate. The reality is that work cultures can be a toxic and dehumanizing place for women because they are frequently up against barriers and hurdles. Women have double the challenge of having to show even more competency and professionalism than their male counterparts. The workforce can genuinely be a cesspool of sexism and discrimination for women. Most of the time, it goes unnoticed and unpunished because speaking out can be a dangerous thing not just in the moment but also for her entire career trajectory.

Women are also not nearly as represented in senior positions. The numbers for women of color in leadership positions also continue to remain low. While progress has been made in recent years, the gap continues to remain startlingly wide between the number of men in senior positions versus women. While so many factors continue to shape our workforce's statistics, it certainly brings up questions about how exactly the gap between men and women in the force has maintained itself and why improvements are moving at a snail's pace.

While there are ways for women to cope with this and try to work around the workforce's disadvantages, the sheer fact that women have to face a set of challenges that males do not encounter is unacceptable and demoralizing. The situation becomes doubly challenging with working mothers who have to deal with a full plate at work and home as well, where their children and the household awaits. Even though the support and resources to help alleviate some of the stress and responsibilities have improved in recent years, access to these resources is not universal. For many families, support is a luxury. Daycare and after-school activities can be an added financial burden that households are not ready for.

As a whole, these dynamics and competing forces are difficult to grapple with. The question or challenge that begs to be answered is how women can find careers that have a positive work environment, fit their skillset, and pay enough while also allowing them to grow and flourish as an individual? It is an incredibly complicated question that continually proves to be an impossible feat for young adults everywhere as the job market grows increasingly competitive and job security looks precarious, at best.

In the workplace and to finally succeed with a career of their own, women are often advised to be more aggressive, adopt male colleagues' habitus, and leave emotions aside to play in the "Boys Club" on the upper floor. This is often meant nicely but overlooks a severe problem: Even if women adopt all-male colleagues' behavior one-to-one, they are assessed differently. If a loud colleague is assertive and "management material," a woman who gets noisy from time to time is quickly described as "bitch" and "too emotional." These assessments are wildly unfair, of course. Still, the deeper issue at hand is that it perpetuates stereotypes about women and is an unjust judge of their character as an individual.

Nevertheless, you can use a few tricks to climb the corporate ladder and sell your achievements well. How does it work? With daring, a good network, and a certain amount of audacity. This book will present to you how you can make a career.

INSIDER TIPS

1. Just do not be too hardworking.

Doing as much as possible well and diligently is still seen by many as the means of choice to attract attention in the job and be seen as a high performer. But that could be the wrong path, says executive coach Christina. She advises women to shift down a gear: "Male monocultures love female diligence because it saves them work. But from experience, I can say that diligent removal sends the wrong signals," she writes in the Handel Blatt.

Successful managers know that just 20% effort is enough to solve 80% of the problems.

Christina, therefore, advises women not to call out "here" when standard tasks are assigned. "Women are much more successful when they pick up strategically important topics or proactively develop them themselves." In this way, women build up an essential field of expertise on the job, which improves their standing and is recognized within the group. Nothing is more crucial than repeatedly pointing out your performance and putting your expertise in the spotlight.

If a female is just getting started with their job fresh from graduation, then they need to keep this in mind: "Do not be too fast on volunteering your help or working too hard to impress your bosses. Be strategic instead." The solution often lies in working smarter, not harder.

2. Women must sell themselves better

Only those who are seen win. Women should therefore use the stage whenever they are available and not skip a presentation. This requires a good deal of self-confidence - and in addition to professional competence, the security to shine and shine with your topic. The best way to do this is through repeated practice: in front of colleagues, in meetings, and in important meetings. Instead of letting others go first, women must take the floor and present themselves.

As a young adult or fresh graduate woman, you might be shy to make a presentation in the front, which should not be. Relinquish that shyness because the competition is high in a place where women should never sell themselves short.

Gone are the days where women are docile and stay hidden behind men. Women should now take a stance and aim to better themselves as well. Women should not be afraid to sell their business skills just because men dominate the industry. Skill and talent do not mind any sex or gender. What matters is if the bearer is skilled or not.

3. Take advantage of your strengths.

Everyone has strengths and weaknesses, but the important thing is that you play up to your strengths and take advantage of the skills that make you a valuable and indispensable part of the company. Working on your weaknesses on the side is an excellent strategy to improve and evolve constantly. But the key here is to put yourself out there with your strong suits and rely on them because they can set you apart from everyone else.

For women especially, it can be tempting to compare yourself with others. Comparing your success with others will only set you back and lead you down a path of self-doubt and insecurity. This can also jeopardize relationships because of how you may be projecting these insecurities onto those you are comparing yourself with.

Analyzing others can help you make practical decisions that will help your career. Rather than comparisons, take a more pragmatic approach by assessing your strengths and then assessing others and how they may add to the dynamic in their unique way. This takes the pressure off from yourself to be like your coworkers and instead focuses on the strengths that reaffirm your position and why you are a valuable member who still has room to grow.

CHARACTERISTICS OF A CAREER WOMAN

If you wish to make a career, you must have the courage to take your professional fate into your own hands and sometimes make risky decisions. Even if people keep talking about compatibility, other things inevitably remain on the job when concentrating on your career. Randi Zuckerberg knows that too. The famous Facebook founder's sister says: "Friendships, career, family, fitness or enough sleep: choose three of them. More is not possible."

Include determination and a willingness to take risks. These qualities also help to climb the corporate ladder:

- Self-discipline
- Courage to be honest
- Assertiveness
- Optimism
- flexibility
- Resilience
- Result orientation
- Openness
- Teamwork

INTERVIEW ANSWERS

What is essential is the desire to have a career

Ms. J, you claim that women appear too modest and sell themselves poorly. Why?

Cornelia J: Women often have little regard for their achievements and do not self-confidently appear as above-average performers. Women also live in more complex life situations: whether at work, as a mother, as a partner, or as a family organizer, many women want to fill all roles optimally. That takes strength. Men, on the other hand, target more on their job. This is noticed by superiors and has lots of advantages.

So, is it their fault if they fail to climb the corporate ladder?

Not exactly. But top management candidates are mostly selected by top management and owners, and most of them are men. Their perception of women in top positions is very different. Also, certain role expectations must be fulfilled in top management, for which women are often poorly prepared.

What expectations?

Fast decision-making, for example. Many male executives do not think long about the consequences of decisions, while women consider their social impact choice. Besides work, the social aspect is also essential: men spend five evenings in a row with customers, women hardly socialize after work or on the weekend. This is because they are still primarily responsible for the household - and men do too little for it.

Experts say that women in management positions bring companies forward economically. Nevertheless, only one in ten managers in Austria is female.

Classic roles continue to dominate in this country. The woman's job is still seen as a side income.

What kind of education or training do women have at work?

It is essential to have a profound desire to have a career. Women must be aware that they must do without a lot for this. That is why when a woman lands her first job after graduation; she needs to have a goal. She needs to acquire as much training as work allows because this training will help to achieve more.

Does a woman have to do more professionally than a man?

Women not only have to perform above average, but they also must sell themselves particularly well to make a career. To get into really top positions, they also must learn how to use power. In many cases, however, there is a lack of role models for this. But that does not mean that it is already time to give up with the lack of role model. No! Instead, women should strive even more to become a pioneer of that change.

In which industries do women have the best chances for a top position?

From today's perspective in service professions. This is where women are mostly socializing and are most likely to be recognized. They are service and customer-oriented, pay attention to their employee's and stakeholders' involvement, and can do many things at once - or at least that is what you believe of them.

NETWORKING FOR YOUR CAREER

Men have recognized it for centuries: their career is not decided in the office but in an informal setting. Whether in the men's toilet or at a company event, a good network is still the be-all and end-all of career planning. Here jobs and projects are assigned informally, and information is shared that bystanders do not even hear or only hear much later. Women who want to get to the top should take this to heart: In an interview with the German star, Douglas M, who calls on women to give each other suitable jobs. "Men have always supported one another. We can do that too!" Said the top manager.

Networking is not a skill that is taught at school. The real, exclusive way to get better at networking is by socializing, which we as humans get better at through experience. Networking, at its core, is a matter of allying. For women, this tends to prove more valuable and necessary than an individual's position or salary. Developing a foundation of mutual respect and trust with a group will grow into a bond that can be extremely valuable in advancing your career. Having people that you can trust in a dog-eat-dog world can make all the difference.

For both men and women, the nature of industries and work environments can often steer them into an increasingly competitive approach to climbing the ladder. Instead of uplifting others, the temptation to step on others to advance is not only tempting but a common occurrence. But doing so enables the toxic environment that continues to not only pit women against each other but also stereotypes women as ruthless, cunning, and altogether unapproachable.

This is where alliances can shape a woman's role in the industry. Having the support of others on a long-term basis can flourish into personal friendships that bleed into personal and professional lives. These contacts are not merely tools for advancing in your career but can become valuable support systems for advice and professional help. Especially in male-dominated industries, this help is central to success.

With men fully taking advantage of networking, as "Boys Only" clubs are rampant in every industry sector, women should weaponize this, just as men have to facilitate their career aspirations and needs. Having the ability to rely on a support group is one of the biggest perks of employment, no matter what industry you are in. Work culture is one of the biggest concerns when it comes to starting a new job. One of the most common questions that interviewers are asked is how the work culture is within the company. For women, this is often coded about the toxicity with other women and the dynamics between genders. It has such a profound impact on every aspect of being an employee and the work they produce. Therefore, having strong ties with like-minded people who also share the same values in terms of the workplace can propel your career and make your experience a far more positive one.

Developing contacts and allowing your qualifications to shine through which can get you into places you may never have even considered before. Networking is useful precisely for this. Building new relationships and getting your name out there exposes you to a larger pool of people who can truly broaden your horizons. This can be a daunting task, but being unafraid and putting yourself out there is the most significant part of networking. Many people fumble during their first few experiences with coffee chats because they tend to psych themselves out. There tends to be considerable stress or pressure that comes with networking, and rightfully so. For many people, the next coffee chat could mean a new opportunity like a promotion or a different position that aligns with their personal goals. You truly can never fully anticipate the extent of the options that arise out of socializing and putting yourself out there.

One of the biggest mistakes that stem from networking anxiety is that people are tempted to overthink things and feel the need to embellish themselves to sell themselves and leave a lasting impression. Ultimately, you are trying to show others your competency, enthusiasm, and qualifications in a more personable and approachable way than in a formal interview setting. This doesn't mean that you have to change your personality and pretend to be someone else entirely. You want to share your authentic self in an organic way, which is often the basis of how these conversations end up turning into networking opportunities that lead to even more options that change a person's career trajectory for the better.

You do not fundamentally have to go to evening events to network. Networking is everywhere: in the coffee kitchen, at the edge of a conference, in the fitness center, or on the playground. To get to know new perspectives and make your competence public, you can always lunch with colleagues from other departments and talk about your projects. After all, everyone is themselves an ambassador for their performance process. That does not mean showing off success at random but instead allowing your expertise to flow in where it is needed - elegantly and as if on the side.

SMART WAYS TO EXPAND YOUR NETWORK

There are also smart ways to set up and expand your network in a targeted manner away from the office lounge.

- **Networking in crowds**: Anyone who loves large groups and quickly gets into a conversation with new people is in good hands at trade fairs and conferences. Alternatively, you can expand a network in workshops or training courses: In small groups, interaction is more manageable, and you automatically have a topic of conversation.
- **Networking from the couch**: Business topics can be discussed, and allies found via Facebook, Twitter, or Xing. This is particularly easy in Facebook groups: They are available on a wide variety of topics and are guaranteed to find like-minded people with whom you can later discuss one or the other business idea in real life over an after-work drink. Another brilliant tool that can get the ball rolling is LinkedIn. Many careers and essential professional relationships have

begun with little research and a quick private message sent through LinkedIn. It's an excellent way to broaden your horizons from the contacts you already have and seek out more like-minded people.

- **Give and take is the cardinal rule in networking**. Anyone who demands without being able to offer something in return is likely to be lost for now. Better: make contacts without obligation and see if you can help where needed. Whether directly in a conversation or later by email or via social media: With information, a contact, or an insider tip, you can make yourself popular, and at some point, you can rely on someone who wants to return the favor. It makes sense to communicate your interests and career plans - this is the only way for the network to know exactly what you are looking for.
- **The network must be in place before it is even needed**. If you are looking for a job at the last minute through someone you have just met, you will not get a hit. Networking only pays off if you have built it up early enough and followed the rules of giving and taking. You should also analyze your

network repeatedly: What are the main focuses, where is someone still missing? Here, specific contacts can be made, and the web can be expanded in a meaningful way.

- **Important: Quality comes before quantity.** This is the only way to stay in touch with your contacts and help each other out. Instead of chasing down as many business cards as possible, the targeted search for one or two contacts per event pays off more. Especially if you want to integrate people into your network in the long term, it is worth looking for people who also suit you personally and appear likable.
- **Stay updated by leveraging your online presence.** Keeping your online resume updated is an excellent way to keep your connections alive, as well as attract new ones. Recruiters can stumble on your profile just by chance. A potential contact may find your page through a mutual contact. There are so many explanations, but the fact stands that social media is a great socializing tool to put yourself out there and start a meaningful relationship with someone who can help you out.

FINALLY, A SALARY THAT SUITS ME

Men still demand higher salaries than women and prefer to negotiate. Charm and modesty are adornments but do not help you in salary negotiations: Here, it is essential to stand up for your value and pay. We will show you how women overcome internal and external resistance and get more out of salary negotiations. Downplaying your value as an employee allows companies to take advantage of you, especially if you are fully qualified to be earning as much as the males in your position. A gender pay gap exists, and part of the reason is that women are less likely to negotiate their salary when offered a job.

How to start negotiating your salary:

- The ability to negotiate your salary depends on your job. Specific jobs tend to have fixed pay rates. This means that negotiating your salary is not on the table for this position. These roles include entry-level jobs and retail or customer service jobs, among others.
- If you are in a mid to higher-level position, compensation tends to get more competitive as you slowly make your way up the career

ladder. This is where discrepancies tend to get pretty obvious when it comes to a gender pay gap.

- Be aware of gender differences. Considering these discrepancies with gender pay is an excellent tactic to use when it comes to negotiating and countering offers. Play it smart and play it cool when it comes to asking your employer for better pay.
- Let the work you have done speak for itself. Quantify your accomplishments and be assertive as you can prove your competency and ability to perform in this role that warrants a salary raise truly. Take an analytical look at all of your accomplishments, and be sure to employ them as you make your case to your boss. This is where all of your efforts accumulate as they attempt to come together and form a decisive decision on whether you deserve a raise or not.
- Show improvement. Showing that you are making a note of the feedback that is being left and using it to improve your performance even further indicates that you are valuable. You continue to be advantageous because

you are always improving yourself to suit the needs of the company.
- Stop apologizing. This goes for women in any aspect of their professional life, whether about asking for a raise or a colleague's favor. Apologizing only puts a target on your back and tells people that you are meek and a pushover. Prefacing things with "I'm so sorry to bother you" "or "I feel bad asking this" takes power away from your words and removes the intent out of apologizing when you do it too many times.
- Be diplomatic. No matter what the outcome is, maintain your professionalism and keep yourself contained. If you have been rejected, the best way is to take this as a learning experience that you can consider the next time you think it is opportune to ask for a raise.

TOO NICE FOR THE JOB?

For too long, loudness has been equated with self-confidence and assertiveness. Studies show that young employees, graduates, and young professionals have long since stopped feeling like bosses who sometimes get loud when things do not go as they want. In the meantime, empathy and sympathy are the criteria that make a good manager - and that women are often ascribed to based on their gender.

So, everything is okay? Yes and no. Even those who are quiet, friendly, and nice must know what they - or she - want. Otherwise, the team will run in a direction that will not help anyone. So, while the days of roaring bosses are over and cooperation on equal terms is on the agenda, people are still needed who have a vision of where the journey should go - and who says that it must be a man? Women can do the same.

CAREER AND CHILD TOGETHER – IS THIS POSSIBLE?

This is the age-old question that plagues women around the world. Having a career and a child seems like water and oil, and many industries treat it as such. Women who are invested in their careers but manage to run a family are often told that they "have it all," which cannot be farther from the truth. Having a work-life balance is difficult when you are a full-time employee, but adding motherhood into the mix only complicates things. If you thought you didn't have time before, wait until you have kids.

The fact is that women are always sacrificing themselves to be at multiple places at once. This means missing out on certain things at each end of the spectrum. Working for long hours at work and then coming home to care for children is beyond exhausting and a Herculean task for most.

The time-out on parental leave does not necessarily have to mean the end of a woman's career - provided she take care of it. Even if it is nice to accompany the new life, thoughts about the office should find space. In the first few months of parental leave, the contact is still maintained, but after six months at the latest, women must work hard to stay on the ball professionally.

That works: With weekly meetings, part-time employment in addition to parental leave or telephone conferences in which women can keep up to date with the current state of affairs. After the baby break, many women return to part-time jobs - and thus miss another career opportunity. Presentism is still firmly anchored in many offices: those who are not physically sitting on their office armchair are de facto absent.

It is advisable to take on self-sufficient projects that are regularly presented and discussed. They can often be allocated more flexibly in terms of time and show the employer that there is still enough strength for the job - and the will to do that little bit extra for the company.

In the long term, the compatibility of work and private life is an issue that affects both genders, even if many employers still see it intensely on the part of the mothers. Fathers, who take care of a child break themselves and then share the care obligations, are generous support - and women must also actively demand them.

WHAT WOMEN WHO MADE IT SAY

Young female founders know how it has done: They have created companies out of nothing successfully in the market. In an interview with the German Huffington Post, they advise women who want to pursue a career, among other things, to strengthen networking and employ mentors - and explain why it is sometimes better for your job if you do not even know what you are getting yourself into.

Tijen O from the Women network advises women to make themselves visible and work on a self-marketing strategy that clarifies what they stand for. Whether via your blog, via social media, or in networks such as Xing or LinkedIn, anyone who establishes themselves as an expert on a topic automatically has an excellent professional standing.

Güncem C advises women to approach career planning strategically. "The job depends on other things than just hard work," says the superwoman. Endless overtime does not get anyone any further - networking skills and soft skills such as empathy and listening are much more critical. Güncem advises every woman to listen to herself: What are her strengths and weaknesses? On this basis, she should find a mentor to work with her on her development. "That would certainly have helped me in the first few years. That's why I like to support young women in their jobs."

Ida T is one of the few women who have ventured into the health tech industry. She wants to break down gender biases in the startup industry and pave the way for other women to get there. "No woman should ever hesitate to ask for help. Only if we support each other in our endeavors will women become stronger and will assert themselves - regardless of the industry, "says Ida. The ideas or yourself do not have to be perfect. The main thing is to start. "Not knowing what you're getting into at the beginning of your career is a great gift."

Christina B and her husband founded the Shiftschool in 2016, Germany's first academy for digital transformation. For them, the essential prerequisite for a successful career is the ability to take on responsibility in the job and work through topics from A to Z. "It is precious when the boss can rely on employees who are responsible for something to make decisions themselves and to stand by them. Then the boss can delegate with a clear conscience," says Christina. But it is also essential for a career to learn to believe in yourself and to trust yourself. Reflecting on the challenges you have already mastered in your life gives you strength. "Tell yourself: I can do this; I've already done completely different things."

Antonia A developed the Careship company and her brother and said: Women must not allow themselves to be dissuaded from their path and dreams - and not from anyone. "The eagerness to jump into the deep end, and also to take risks and to work with incomplete information has brought me a long way in my career." In her opinion, women should trust themselves more and learn to sell themselves well.

RESPONDING TO PEOPLE WHO SAY YOU CANNOT MAKE IT AS A WOMAN

Being a woman comes with great responsibility and, at some point - more significant setbacks. This is more so if you are a young woman. In the workplace, in any industry, at home, with peers, women find themselves in situations where others question their capabilities just because they are women. 4 out of 5 women receive sexist and offensive remarks.

You will come across people bothered by your gender or your greatness as you start working at any point in life. But do not cower in dismay because you can do something about it. Read on to find out how.

Keep Your Composure

First things first, as a young adult on the first day of work, keep your composure. Do not feel intimidated by the people at work and their insignificant opinions, and do not let it consume you. That is just what it is - a mere opinion. Reacting emotionally or defensively can only exacerbate the situation. Do not attach bearing to words that come from strangers and rude strangers at that.

Furthermore, do not attach these opinions to your competency or value as an individual. The important thing is to differentiate between constructive criticism and criticism that is entirely unwarranted and unnecessary. Doing so will set you up for success because constructive criticism can help you improve and evolve as an individual, employee, and team player.

But when it comes to people who are only looking to pass judgments about you, understand where they are coming from and remember that it is a place of insecurity from seeing a woman thrive and succeed where they were not able to. Many charlatans will underestimate your abilities. But that is just a projection of what they are – intimidated by how far you can come and how much you can achieve. Filter the words you listen to, the ones you allow to influence how you think and what you do.

Know the Motive

You can think of a way to respond when you know

your detractor's motive behind the denigration. Yes, it is ironic, but a way to understand how to respond better is understanding why. Negative criticisms are projections of an underlying inferiority complex.

It says more about the person than about you. They may feel threatened by your power, or they are not willing to learn under you. They also want to be at par with you, but they know they just cannot. Shame with a hint of anger may have also prompted the affront.

Understanding their motives can help you reconfigure their words to be far less hurtful because, ultimately, we are human beings with feelings. You will feel attacked, and the urge to get defensive will make itself known. But the fact is, knowing that their attacks come from their underlying insecurities helps you see that the fault does not indeed lie within yourself.

Retaliate when Ready

There is nothing wrong with retaliating, especially if you are the affected one. However, not all vilifiers warrant your response. You need not explain. If they only want to shake your confidence and have nothing worthwhile to spend their time on, better not invest yours in getting back at them.

Silence is an act of better revenge. It takes a sheer amount of courage and conviction to counter your critic's disapproval. But you do not always have to. It is a way to get the message across that you are a woman of purpose whose time you invest only in your commitments and the things that matter. Better let your success be your indignant statement.

Call them out and Discourse

When men's affront are out of bounds, pull them up on their sexism and engage them in a conversation. Make them realize that gender is not a measure of competence. See, many women are now on the rise, and in fact, some are in leadership positions. It is a golden reason to take pride in your being. Being a woman is not a mistake. It is a strength, so do not apologize nor explain. Your identity as a woman is your answer.

When others denigrate you just because you are a woman, mostly young, keep your calm and collect your thoughts. Never stoop down to their level. Show them that gender is not a measure of competence, and success knows no sex. In-home life and the work-place, women are the masters of commitment, so there is absolutely no reason for the belittling.

11 CAREER TIPS WITH GUARANTEED SUCCESS

✓ **More courage with applications**: It is perfectly okay to apply for job advertisements whose requirements are only met by 60-70%.

✓ **Enter the competition**: It does not always have to be faster, higher, and further: Smart solutions often lead to more than sheer muscle power.

✓ **Appreciate your performance**: What you have achieved is worth a lot - you can be proud and build on it.

✓ **Mathematics, science, and sport**: women can do everything they want, even if clichés often suggest the opposite.

✓ **Make financial demands**: no woman must be satisfied with what she has.

✓ **Negotiating**: Whether salary or area of responsibility: You can learn to negotiate - and sometimes it is even fun.

✓ **Pushing for promotion**: If it does not work the first time, stick with it: A follow-up interview a few months later often brings the desired result.

✓ **Support bosses**: For networks function, prejudices must get support from the head and women in their team's management positions.

✓ **Get the best of both worlds**: "Male" characteristics such as power-conscious, assertive, and self-confident work wonders in conjunction with "female" attributes such as communicative, diplomatic, and sensitive.

✓ **Look for a managerial position**: should someone else look after the household and children. Women are now making a career.

✓ **Praise yourself**: Nobody gets bored talking about their strengths

SIX TIPS ON HOW YOU CAN MAKE A CAREER AS A YOUNG WOMAN

Career advancement is not only reserved for men. The tips reveal how you can make a career as a young woman.

There are many career planning guides out there that cater to both men and women. But women who wish to make a career should avoid a few pitfalls so that the way up does not end in a dead-end. But how can you successfully circumnavigate these cliffs? Here are six tips that should help you to develop a career as a woman.

Tip 1 - do not present yourself as a glamorous girl!

Do not fight with the woman's arms! You are not there to seduce your boss; instead, you plan to take his post someday. Even if you have a flawless figure: mini-skirt and deep necklines do not belong in the workplace.

Better this way: Wear costumes and combine them with colored tops and scarves. Go to the hairdresser and apply make-up discreetly. You are a woman, after all!

The counterpart to the glamour girl, the hard-working grey mouse who hopes that her performance will be noticed and rewarded, but is practically invisible, will not have a career.

Ultimately, being comfortable in your skin brings about the confidence that simply cannot be replicated.

So, while it is important to dress professionally and appropriately, that does not mean that you cannot have a personality.

Tip 2 - Present your work confidently

Women tend to view humility as the highest virtue. That is counterproductive in professional life! Do not make yourself smaller than you are! Once you start, after graduation, flaunt your accomplishments to decision-makers.

Your work is an extension of you. You want your efforts to go noticed because they attest to your abilities and competencies. By presenting your work confidently, you signify to everyone in the room that you want their attention on the work you have done. Being meek only leads people to think that your appointment is not up to par and is not worth spending time on.

When you are praised, take it for granted. For example, answer: "Yes, I got the project off well; there is a lot of work behind it." You may then immediately follow up with a question about promotion or a salary increase.

Tip 3 - Use your social skills but do it properly!

If you want to make a career as a young woman, you have something decisive ahead of men, namely higher social skills. Because women are more communicative, they can grasp moods in individuals or groups more quickly and react appropriately. Therefore, the participation of women in disputes has a balancing effect because their contributions contain compromises, which leads to more constructive results than if the men attack each other like gamecocks.

The other side of the coin: Don't become the department's suggestion box for sheer empathy. Also, do not accept that your colleague will pass work onto you because of lovesickness. Postpone private calls to breaks and after work!

Tip 4 – Contribute to meetings

On no occasion do men and women behave as obviously different as they do in business meetings. Not only do men speak up significantly more often, but they also do so with self-confidence that often cannot be objectively justified. If you want to make a career as a woman, you must catch up with men on this point. So, hands up and speak out before your colleague does! It is best to have an introductory sentence ready if it is your turn. And not "I would think" or "maybe it could be that" (typically feminine formulations) but "I believe," "the fact is," or "it is clear that."

Tip 5 - the "family trap."

That is the most delicate point. When applying, women, unlike men, are often asked whether they are planning to start a family. If you want to have a career as a woman, you must clarify that work has a top priority. Better to avoid words like "part-time" or "back off." Then, when there is indeed a baby, you will not need to be feeling guilty. You are not a bad mother if your child is well looked after, including by you, but not around the clock.

Tip 6 - learn to talk

Did you do a good job? Then stand by it and show it with exact words. Anyone who wants to fill a management position must be able to give good speeches. This is the only way to convince. Having strong public speaking capabilities can set you apart in a room full of noise. Not only are you far more eloquent and well-thought-out, but you also come off well-prepared and knowledgeable. Remember, leaving a lasting impression can assert your role in the room and beyond.

HOW TO DEAL WITH DISCRIMINATION AT THE WORKPLACE FOR WOMEN

Society favors you if you are not a woman. A challenging, cold, dismaying fact that exists in the workplace today. Discrimination against women may come in all forms - being paid relatively less, harassed by words and action, or denying the opportunity or promotion they deserve.

If you are a woman with such experience, rise from that place of silence that only benefits your oppressors. But first, you need to know when an act or a remark is a sign of discrimination.

Equalrights.org outlines the many forms of discrimination with legal bearing and could earn the perpetrators a one-way ticket to court. Discrimination includes the following.

- Denied a position in the workplace because of your gender
- Receiving a lower salary compared to male counterparts

- Being evaluated on a more stringent standard or criteria
- Penalized for not conforming to standards
- Refrained from opportunities like training, promotion, or a pay raise
- Forced to pick up the slack or quit because you are young and a woman
- You are being insulted and called derogatory slurs and names.

Courage will breed from knowledge. It perceives when it is time to stand up and how it is crucial. Read on to know what else you can do once you find yourself on the receiving end of assault or prejudice.

Know Your Rights

- It is your right to work in a fair and safe space and an environment free from discrimination.
- You can express your thoughts on discrimination and your intentions to foster a safe, discrimination-free environment for you and your colleagues. You can pull people into the conversation and eventually mitigate such a pressing issue. Know that it is illegal

for the employer to penalize you for doing so.
- It is your right to report to your immediate superiors or the human resource personnel about any form of harassment you experience at work.
- If your employer reduces or withholds your salary, fires you from work, or demotes you for doing these things, you can sue under these grounds. Note that any form of retaliation from your employer is illegal.

Document Your Experience

On the onset, write every experience, every word, or action done in an assault. It may not be as easy as it sounds, but this will help support your complaints later. Keep them objective and factual as much as possible. Keep records of messages, e-mails, or pictures for you to use when needed. Pen down the names of witnesses and their contact numbers. When your employer retaliates at you, record every detail and keep them in a place or electronic storage where only you or people you trust can access.

Review Policies of the Workplace

Look for the companies' policies regarding discrimination. Study the procedures you need to undergo if you experience the same, the necessary steps to take when raising a complaint, and the people you need to consult with your concern. Keep a record of their contact numbers and requirements in case the need arises.

Report to Your Higher-ups

Armed with the knowledge of the complaint procedures, you can report your situation to your boss, or your HR. Equalrights.org suggests that you commit your complaint into writing, whether by letter or e-mail and keep several copies for proof. When you face discrimination as a woman, do not let their intimidation or your fear silence you. Deal with it head-on and take action as mentioned above. Always be on guard and keep track of your experience. Women, especially fresh grads and young adults, must hold their ground and stand up until the workplace completely eradicates discrimination and leaves no room for double standards

CAREER ADVICE FOR GRADUATES:
WHAT SHOULD I BE?

Which job is right for me?

Many young people ask themselves this question after completing their studies and training. They are often overwhelmed by the numerous training opportunities, fields of study, job profiles, and their environment's expectations. For fear of a wrong decision, either none is made at all, or they choose the path that their parents have planned for them.

This is a terrifying time because the pressure to have absolutely every detail mapped out is hugely stressful for young people. The question itself is often brought up in interviews: "Where do you see yourself in five years?" Can most people honestly answer that question fully? The answer is no, and most people do not have a fully fleshed-out plan that defines their trajectory for the next five years of their life. Many have a general idea. There is no denying that. But the fact still stands that the expectation is doubled for recent graduates. For young people, this becomes an expectation in and of itself the minute they graduate. The next steps, ambitions, and plans have to be completely figured out to move on from being a student and into the next stage of their lives, which is now a workforce member.

Am I striving for recognition, power, or independence? Does competition or status motivate me? Am I a team, squad player, or a loner? And: who are my role models? Who can I learn from? Who can support me in deciding on a career? These questions are essential when looking for the right job.

We have the answers in this book, and it will help you in intensive one-on-one conversations

- recognize your skills, needs, and values,
- to strengthen trust in you,
- find out which life motives and family characteristics are essential and useful for your professional life,

- develop a concrete plan - with clear and individual strategies for your career choice.

CAREER ENTRY AFTER GRADUATION

After graduating from university, there are various options for taking up a job. Preparing early and looking for a job makes the transition from studying to work easier.

When you have graduated from your university, you will enter the ocean of career seekers to be a part of a dynamic work sector. One factor you must prepare yourself for is intense rivalry from other career-seekers. Because you have only come from a university and no structured job experience to render you the top pick for jobs, it might be complicated.

But do not let this rob you of your faith. Suppose you are at a point where you are always learning to improve your abilities in the industry. There are strategies to become highly employable even though you are a recent graduate. Consider these strategies to take advantage of and outperform other existing professionals.

Training Program

HR departments, government agencies, and recruiting companies embrace emerging technology, including the usage of job-hunting sites and LinkedIn or Facebook Jobs, for posting training programs.

Take time to visit these pages to see what sites publish further work openings or which businesses have earned constructive input from career-seekers. Then build profiles on your preferred worksites and provide your full profile.

Now you should start partaking in the program, completing it, and finally searching for work, based on employers ready to hire new graduates.

Internship

You might run across employers that favor seasoned applicants over young graduates to gain unique skillsets that can only be established over time.

To support you get out of these skills shortages, you should grab the opportunity of the community's internship or volunteering programs. These workshops may offer valuable exposure and experience in critical fields, namely, project management or skills enhancement.

Often, even though they plan to recruit you formally in their company, they will act as a kick-starter to launch your career.

Direct Entry

Your first work prospect does not need to originate from a fair profession. You can prefer to be cautious about seeking a job or employer when you take advantage of your contacts, such as relatives, colleagues, advisors, and those who may be willing to recommend you to possible recruiters or organizations.

Let the people on your network realize that you are searching for career openings. Alternatively, you may want to study businesses where you want to work, as well as notifying your social media friends to inquire about job opportunities in a similar industry.

You will also have to venture through the correct channels to submit, but your edge has already had some favorable opportunities.

Feeling demotivated? Here is how you can handle it

Do not forget what constructive thoughts will bring for your work search efforts. The change from a university existence to a productive hardworking person may render you feeling drained, demotivated, or challenged.

Although this feeling is legitimate, you must remain centered on your job goals— read insightful blogs and books, refresh your website, practice answering typical questions, and more. The plan here is to create a concrete plan for everything that you will do.

Landing the first career opportunity is not as daunting as you believe it is. Take advantage of these tools to help you become as successful as any other applicant in the industry, regardless of the degree of expertise.

Once you have landed your first career opportunity, it is also important to remember that even though your first job may not be your first choice, it certainly does not define your career for the rest of your life. First jobs are a great stepping-stone to the career path you genuinely aspire for, even if the work seems to not align with your ambitions. The vital thing to remember or bear in mind here is that it is a relevant experience, which is tremendously valued as job markets grow increasingly competitive.

Rather than looking at your first job or internship critically, look at it from the lens of what practical skills you can learn and take to your next appointment. Too often do young people get extremely disheartened because they are in a role that they were not necessarily gunning for. But the experience, especially one relevant to the field you are interested in, is crucial for a young person. Showing diverse work history and an advanced skill set can bring you even more opportunities as you choose to advance in your career.

Good luck with your potential career!

JOB QUALIFICATION PROGRAMS

Job qualification programs are vocational certificates for fresh university graduates, also an aspect of the success in landing a job in an industry. They are typically related to a specific sector and are structured to strengthen and acquire the necessary skills for your career route.

Benefits of Qualification Programs

Through qualification programs, you will gain the following benefits:

- Eligibility to work
- Strengthening your CV
- Gaining professional status
- Learning new skillsets
- Promotion

How to Find Qualification Programs

To become qualified in your preferred occupation, you must first find a suitable industry. Then, you would often go through a process to fulfill a technical qualification. For example, whether you wish to be a certified accountant or engineer.

Typically, if you choose to be a part of a formal association or institution, you will still need to be certified. As a consequence, the bulk of technical certificates are approved by professional entities.

For instance, several graduates who wish to become certified accountants would prepare for an Institute of Chartered Accountants in England and Wales or ICAEW certification.

Things to Consider When Looking for the Right Program

Most industries have some form of industry-specific certifications or technical qualifications, so selecting a related industry is essential. It is not about the regular suspects, namely judges, surgeons, and attorneys, who train for professional licensures. For instance, you can receive specialist certificates in fields such as advertisement, sales, banking, and sport.

Additionally, you should also consider the time of completion. It may take a couple of weeks and a few years to acquire such technical credentials. Flexibility is also the secret to accomplishing a technical course since most career pursuers study while employed full-time. So, many technical classes are either part-time or delivered by distance learning.

Look for the skillsets that you need to learn in a job qualification program. Most of the main graduation plans, school leavers services, and training programs require their interns to strive for a distinct technical degree while at the same time obtaining on-the-job immersion.

While entry-level programs are usually free for fresh graduates, any specialist credentials can be costly, just like the LPC. Probably, you are going to have to find out whether it is a wise expenditure or not. However, the employer may be in a role to support or contribute to the bill. For example, in hindsight, individual law firms would pay the LPC's expense for any trainees they take on.

The level of commitment is also one of those things that you need to consider. You would still need to decide whether it is worth spending time and dedication to gain a technical certification or not. Is it going to improve your career? Is it going to get you additional attention or increase your salary? Many students waste money on the acquisition of a technical degree before they even get a promising job.

When enrolling in a technical qualification course, verify that the certification you earn is related to your career, and confirm that a professional entity exists. The main thing to note is that a well-chosen technical certificate could boost your chances of getting employed amongst all other benefits.

HOW TO PREPARE FOR YOUR FUTURE JOB AS A STUDENT

Preparing for your future job as a student is crucial. It is a better investment of your time than throwing parties and getting distracted. There is nothing wrong with having fun but remember that the real world has high expectations for the new workforce. As early as you can, build your resume. You can also try these tips to be a valuable asset in your future company.

Choice of specializations

Choose the career that you do not mind doing for decades. Let it be something that aligns with your interests and lucrative enough to sustain your needs. In making this decision, you need self-awareness and knowledge of your desired career to guide you. Pick the specialization that suits your aptitudes and skills lest you dread your work each time. Set realistic expectations and work on the skills you need for the job.

Voluntary study internships

You can do your research about the career paths you are interested in. You can read about them, but nothing beats a hands-on learning experience. Sign up for internships when you can. This will give you a glimpse of the heart of the work. You learn the essentials, the basics in and out of your specialization. You get training and advice from people who have worked for years. You can start with a small business within your community and help them grow.

Project work

Embark on a project you choose for yourself. While you are at it, allow yourself to make mistakes. This is just one of the meaningful ways to learn. The more blunders you make, the better you become at your craft. This is one answer to how you can prepare yourself in the future. Remember that it is a rat race out there in the world. Experience is your armor.

Thesis topic

Another thing you can add to your knowledge is completing a thesis that interests you and you believe is impactful. Choose a thesis topic that reflects your passion so you do not have a hard time writing it. This hones your research skills and your initiative to get the work done. In short, remember these three things 1) list the topics that interest you, 2) sort the issue that you care about researching, and 3) choose the best case that also relates to your chosen specialization.

Part-time employment

You can also search for part-time jobs if you wish to make extra money while gaining experience. Aside from the extra bucks, you acquire the following skills.

- *Time Management*. This is the most given skill you can gain by landing a part-time job. You master how to balance your responsibilities as a student and an employee.
- *Independence*. You learn the right work ethics even under pressure.
- *Financial management skills*. As you are earning, you learn how to manage your money and set aside your expenses and savings.
- *Interpersonal skills*. When you are out there, you are bound to meet people and communicate with them, especially if you are in a place where you provide value to clients or customers.
- *Professional network*. This is a place where you can at least start to build professional connections too. They will be valuable to you as you journey through your work life and post studies.

Voluntary work

Engage with your community and extend your relevant talents. This is also one way to make connections and build meaningful relationships. You can meet people and learn from their experiences related to your career choice. You gain knowledge, hone practical skills, and make an impact at the same time. It is also a bonus for your resume. Learning has no limits, and the ones you gain from hands-on experience equip you better.

Foreign language skills

Communication and public speaking are soft skills you can learn if you commit to them. Learning a foreign language is especially relevant to you if you plan to work abroad. There are apps and free online resources that you can access to aid your learning. Know the country's culture and research information about it in advance, so you do not get lost - literally and figuratively, later.

Specific IT skills

Technology has shaped the systems of the workplace. This is better to be on your list of skills to learn. From the most basic, like writing emails to learning about programming and other software, you can start somewhere. You need not be a master of all; you just need to put in the work and learn the fundamentals.

As a learner, there are a lot of options for you to gain experience and develop your skills. Follow the steps above and leave the room for growth open. Keep your willingness to improve. It will not be too easy, but it will be worth it. You will reap the rewards for the efforts you have put in.

JOB HUNTING TIPS FOR GRADUATES

Being able to get out of college with a hard-fought degree can be very liberating. No more all-nighters, no more crammed reviewing for exams, etc. Though it may seem like you have figured out everything, graduating from college is just a single step towards the real world.

As a graduate, you will be met with responsibilities and obligations like supporting your family or providing food on the table. All these things will only be possible when you land a job. However, this begs the question, "how do I land a job?" Well, here are job hunting tips for graduates like you to consider!

Resumes and Cover Letters

Your degree will likely determine the job you would apply for since it will suit your qualification. Regardless of what you graduate with, whether Latin honors or not, accept that people will most likely not recognize you. That is why you will need to introduce yourself to them first, hence the need for resumes and cover letters.

Resumes are to be understandable and straightforward, but they must capture who you are. HR professionals do not dwell on technical details, so keep it away from jargons. Additionally, highlight the actual contents like your achievements, expertise, and extracurricular activities relevant to the job description.

Cover letters must also follow suit. Begin with introducing yourself and then dwell on your motivation in applying for the job. You must even convince them about why they should hire you, so make sure to mention why you are the perfect person for the job.

Moreover, tell them what you can contribute to their company once you have been hired.

Unsolicited Applications

These applications are a bit different from the previously discussed. There are instances when you take an interest in applying for a job, but there might not be an opening or hiring for an exciting position at the moment. You can still send a letter of application, but it is referred to as an unsolicited one.

The main difference is that this application requires more intensive research on the company or the position. You must be familiar with the employer or the work culture and express sincerity as to why you want to participate in the job. Like solicited applications (has announced job openings), you again must mention how you can be an asset to them.

Declined Applications

Application denials can occur even without the interview taking place yet. When these instances happen, it can be for one of two reasons: there is someone more suitable, or your resume was the problem.

When you continuously apply for work yet get consistent rejections, check your resume and identify what is wrong. It might lack substance. Every application letter must be unique to each company. Keep it short and sweet but make sure to capture them with the carefully selected words you will use.

Interviews

Make an impression. From your attire to the way you answer questions, to the contents of your answer, will determine whether you will get the job or not. Remember that being in an interview means that you can resume work or have an on-paper qualification that has worked. They just need to know you and what you can do.

Plan out what you will be wearing for the interview—something presentable, which will make you feel confident. Plan out your consultation by answering common job interview questions. Create concrete answers in your head. This way, when you sit in front of the recruiter, you will grasp what to say.

First Day

Your first day, ah yes, finally it has arrived. It is not a competition. You do not have to make your boss coffee and clean the bathroom altogether to impress them. You just must do the job description and fulfill what you have promised to offer them during your application.

Ask relevant job questions; this shows curiosity and investment in the job. Prepare to answer questions from colleagues who are asking you about yourself and your previous employments. Everything will be okay. Just smile, relax, familiarize yourself with the work dynamics, and make friends. You will adapt there soon enough.

WHERE TO GET SUPPORT?

Leaping from being a university student to being an employee who must face real-life challenges might be scary at first. Therefore, you need support from experts and the people who genuinely care about you to make this transition as smooth as possible. Here are some places and people you can seek help from in making your transition from being a student to being an employee.

Special literature

This unique literature involves research and articles formulated focusing on a specific topic, and in this case, employment and job opportunities. Do your research and look closely into these kinds of literature. These scholarly articles will provide you with the facts and information like statistics and different studies to help you transition.

Internet

You can also take advantage of the golden era of technology by using the internet and researching various ways on how you can make the transition from being a student to being an employee in a smooth manner. There are countless blogs, podcasts, videos, and tutorials on how you can do this. All you are expected to do is to be resourceful and fact-check your research first before anything else.

Job consultations

Another thing you can do is to seek the help of a consultant. These job consultations aim to answer your questions about making the transition from "student life" to "real life." The viewpoints and opinions you will be hearing will be coming from the experts in the field so you can be sure that it is reliable and accurate.

Mentors

Having a mentor to guide you through anything is one of the best things you can have. Your mentor might be an expert in the field or even just someone who has any experiences that they can relay to you, which in turn can help make your transition smooth and easy. Your mentor might be a close friend who has enough experience or your former professors in school.

Family

Lastly, you can turn to the people who would not charge you fees for their advice and who would provide you with all the love and support they can give as you take the step to another chapter of your life - your family. You can ask your parents or your older siblings how they did it back when they were fresh graduates and were looking for a job.

The transition from being a student who is worried about passing assignments on time and joining various contests to being an employee who must face real-life challenges is hard. Still, it can be made smooth and easy if you only know where to look and seek support. Many people have already experienced what you are about to go through. You just must ask them for guidance and listen to the advice they give.

ADDITIONAL TRAINING?

To get into a job faster or more successfully, some graduates do plan additional training. However, this exclusive makes sense if it is generally required (e.g., medicine) or qualified for a specific function (e.g., high school teacher). However, for most graduates, the first step is to acquire professional experience and not even more theory.

CAREER MANAGEMENT

Career management is the lifelong practice of investing resources to achieve your career goals. Career management is not one event but a continuing process necessary to adapt to the 21st Century economy's changing demands—career Vision's schedule supports ongoing personal and professional development throughout life's transitions.

Even if we are in the early phase of our work life or are workforce veterans, we have probably heard the term career management. We have likewise probably heard that in the future we need to be responsible for our careers. What we may not have n disclosed is what career management is and how we should do it! Career management uses concepts similar to sound financial management. A great rule of thumb to keep in mind is that a disciplined investment, made regularly, yields a greater return. Although the tactics will differ, career management focuses on two critical investment assets to manage throughout our working years, our lifelong personal learning and our network of relationships.

LIFELONG LEARNING

It is often startling to realize how much of our day-to-day work is now based around technology: computers and other scientific advancements, which have radically altered how we conduct our work. The consequence of these advancements and innovations will ripple very swiftly through the economy, obsolescing many businesses and catapulting others into the limelight. How well we can adapt to these ongoing innovations will directly relate to how we keep our knowledge and skills. Consider how to diversify your investments in time, energy, and resources. Examples might incorporate credentialed coursework (locally or through distance learning), topical courses for certificates, joining cutting-edge projects, attending seminars, or staying current in professional reading.

NETWORK OF RELATIONSHIPS

As we have moved to an information and service economy, relationship contacts have become an increasingly critical asset. Not only do our relationships help us accomplish our day-to-day tasks with colleagues, vendors, customers, and competitors, but these relationships will also be the source of information about how fields and industries are evolving. We also have contacts outside of our work environments affiliated with our hobbies, children, spiritual, or community networks. These personal and professional contacts will transcend specific companies, industries, and organizations. How we interact, reply, and connect in all our communications will impact our current performance and future opportunities. Very limited is accomplished in isolation. Networking uncovers more than 71% of current job openings.

Keeping connected with contacts and knowing how to build good relationships is more important than ever before. These skills can be advanced in applied communication courses, mastering contact management software, effective listening, and an honest desire to get to know people better.

Lifelong training, relationship, and contact management form the backdrop of successful career management. Starting a vision and plan are also essential for guiding informed investment decisions and establishing annual goals. The career vision we select should be broad enough to be flexible but definitive enough to be actionable. This career vision, built on a profile of our unique traits, directs our choices to develop what we need to be satisfied and be able to contribute to different work environments over the years successfully. To manage our adaptability and employability, habitually establishing annual learning objectives and nurturing our relationships are the keys to productive career management.

CAREER MANAGEMENT PROCESS

Career Management is a life-long development of investing resources to accomplish your future career goals. It is a continuing development that allows you to adapt to the changing demands of our dynamic economy. Career management development embraces various concepts: Self-awareness, career development, planning/career exploration, life-long learning, and networking.

SELF-AWARENESS

Look at yourself to reveal your interests, skills, personality traits, and values. You can start by asking yourself the questions below:

- Who are you?
- What interests you?
- What do you like to do?
- What are you good at doing?
- What do you value, what is important to you?
- What are your unique assets, skills, and abilities?
- Who requires the talents, skills, and abilities you can provide?
- What work environment and arrangements make sense to you?
- What activities do I find fun, motivating, engaging, and enjoyable?
- What skills do you need to have to develop and manage your career?

- What personal style or peculiarity do I have that are essential to me in the workplace?

Ask friends, colleagues, family members, co-workers, professors, or mentors if they identify the same qualities in you as you see in yourself.

CAREER DEVELOPMENT PLANNING/CAREER EXPLORATION

Career Development Planning is a system designed to help you:

- Take the time to reflect on your job/career goals
- Focus and target on developing knowledge and skills for your current position and future job opportunities
- Think about how you can utilize your strengths, talents, experience, and motivation efficiently – how can you use all these aspects to increase your passion for work!
- Be the architect of your career development plan – write your goals, decide to have a plan for your career development

- Discuss your career process goals with your manager.

Once you have made a career decision or choice, you now need to plan how you will decide. A career plan provides vision, direction, structure, and motivation for your career management process.

WHAT DO YOU THINK OF CAREER PROCESS PLANNING?

Usually, when we think of career management, we think of the goals or action items we need to move our careers forward. Often, we carry some of these thoughts around in our heads for long periods without ever writing them down. If we do pen down our goals, they usually take the form of a list, and many times we lose motivation after writing our goals down, misplace the list, and attain only some of our dreams. That is why this style of thinking and just penning your career objectives is not a very motivating or reinforcing process!

It is far more potent, motivating, and productive to think of career planning as a process that allows us to envision our future careers and then provides us with a path to pursue our goals and realize our dreams. Career planning is not something that happens once or twice in one's career. On the contrary, it is a recurring process of taking the time to assess one's identity, setting new goals, creating new career horizons, and celebrating successes as one develops and becomes more knowledgeable and skilled

CAREER KILLER

*G*ood performance, perseverance, and relationships - with this trio, you will quickly get up the career ladder. But as soon as some climb the steps - they fall just as quickly. Because on the way to the top, some stumbling blocks have messed up their careers. Indeed, mistakes can never be avoided entirely. But your risk becomes smaller when you know these typical career killers. You have already taken the leading step towards this: you are reading this book- and hopefully, you can identify the most common career killers and successfully avoid them.

YOU OBSTRUCT YOUR CAREER

Has a colleague suggested to you a promotion path? Has your career been stagnated? It would be easy now to blame the incompetent boss or the slimy colleague for your failure. But the truth is more uncomfortable: most workers stand in their way as they advance.

Technical competence is only one side of the coin. If you want to get ahead in your job, you must be highly committed, continuously develop yourself, know the game's rules, and perform specific job behaviors. Otherwise, others will pass you by.

Taking responsibility for one's actions and possibly for setbacks is certainly not always easy. You can only consciously avoid frequent career killers and shape your professional future if you take matters into your own hands.

Sometimes even the little things are enough to cause lasting harm or to land in a career impasse. Therefore, do not view the following list of errors as regulations or charges. Instead, it should serve to raise awareness of these potential career killers.

ENDING THE PROMOTION

Endless frustration.

Anyone who sneaks through the office floors with drooping heads, as if they were carrying the company's burden on their shoulders, will soon stomp in the basement. Nobody likes certified fun brakes. Especially not in times of crisis. This calls for types who spread optimism, not an apocalyptic mood.

For you, constant frustration quickly turns into a career killer. If you are always dissatisfied and believe that your career advancement will not work out anyway, it will probably be the same. You can only make a career if others believe in you - but for that to be possible, you must think that you can do it.

Product disappointment.

It is the worst thing a company can do to its customers. Customers have zero tolerance for this and never buy again. Therefore, never make promises that you cannot keep. Neither when taking on a project nor during a promotion, let alone in an interview.

In doing so, you are only fueling unrealistic and harmful expectations. The first time, the self-inflicted disappointment may not seem so bad. But with every subsequent time, it undermines trust in you. They mutate into a blender - without any external compulsion. With all understanding of self-marketing: Don't stack too high, especially at the beginning. There are many advantages to being underestimated - even if it is only that you can surprise business partners, colleagues, and bosses: positively.

Arrogance.

Young colleagues and young professionals believe that it is smart to shine through so much performance that it even puts their boss in the shade. Huge mistake! Those who let their talents shine brighter than those of the boss inevitably arouse their envy and distrust. And that ends badly.

Just watch what happens when someone optimizes the boss's idea with your own in the next meeting. Please just observe, do not try it yourself! That is why true professionals play beyond gangs - they naturally make the boss look smarter than themselves, for example, by asking them for advice. Mighty people are enthusiastic about such requests. Only a boss who has been able to give you the gift of their superiority will protect you permanently.

Advice resistance.

Of course, not every colleague who gives you advice means well. Sometimes it is intrigue, or a wrong track, or an attempt to make yourself bigger as an advisor. However, these are rather exceptions. As a rule, the help you need now can only be found one office away. And it would be stupid not to take advantage of this opportunity.

It is even more stupid not to learn from people who may be further than you and have more experience. Anyone who thinks that this is how they document their independence is making a grave mistake: they remain dependent on their competence and creativity. And that is just not always enough. Often it is only pride that keeps us from doing it - and therefore keeps us small.

If you ask for tips or help, you may feel small at first. In the long run, however, it will surpass itself. And on top of that, it builds a valuable network of advisors and mentors.

False modesty

Modesty is an ornament - you get no further without it: As vain and unpleasant as self-portrayal may seem, whoever does not attract attention falls through the grid. Even the most outstanding achievement fizzles out if nobody notices it. This constant advertising naturally requires a sure instinct; otherwise, it quickly drifts into self-importance.

In your job, you should be wiser. Tried and tested methods provide regular interim reports and progress reports for larger tasks, for example. Or speak up in meetings. Not all the time, but with well-developed, fresh ideas. Or you offer your knowledge and help to other colleagues. This has the advantage that they will talk positively about you later. And word of mouth is even more effective than self-promotion.

Perfectionism.

It is a mistake not to want to make mistakes. Some individuals waste their whole lives trying to do this. Objectively speaking, they may be less likely to make mistakes than others. But they also do less because they spend a lot of time avoiding potential errors. Of course, it is wise to set high standards for yourself and others. But only if they are realistic.

Otherwise, perfectionism will only hold you back. It leads to tunnel vision in which those affected concentrate on details that are of little importance for the big picture. Defects can broaden one's horizons: Without mistakes, Christopher Columbus would never have discovered America. Successful people are characterized precisely by the fact that they make mistakes because they do more than others. An error is not bad if it is not repeated, and you learn from it.

Like the IBM founder Tom Watson, when one of his employees made a severe mistake, it cost him $ 600,000. Watson was then asked if he would fire the employee, which Watson vehemently denied. He just said, I just invested $ 600,000 in his education. Why would anyone else get this experience for free? Note: only gods can afford zero tolerance for errors.

Loquacity.

The cabaret artist Willy Reichert once said: Gossip is the tangible connection between two loose tongues. Many people immediately believe what is whispered. Indiscretion often spreads faster than noise. Insidious!

It is not uncommon for the short-term feeling of superiority to proclaim something that no one knows yet as a Pyrrhic victory. First, because some of the dirt always sticks to the thrower. Second, because blasphemy does not exactly indicate a noble character. Third, because communication may turn out to be untrue, then the author is either considered a liar or an unsuspecting pomposity. Both are bad.

There is hardly anything that damages the career as much as the image of a localized leak. King Solomon warned his pupils: Anyone who acts as gossip is divulging secrets. So, do not get involved with someone who talks a lot.

Stubbornness.

Every company has its own culture. Behind it are often unwritten rules for dealing with one another, for procedures in meetings, language codes, or reporting chains. It is good not to leave the office before 7 p.m. Others always take their department for lunch or hand out coffee and cake on their birthday.

Still, others see poor elbow use as a sign of weakness. No matter how much you insist on your individuality: Playing along is a must. Or they'd better look for a different team and company. Such behavior patterns are always also a kind of immunity test: Those who cannot assimilate into the organism will soon be rejected.

Job starters do well to find out quickly which rules are being played and worked by. The best strategy for the first few weeks: listens carefully, watch - and shut up.

Self-doubt. (Permanent)

If you are one of those people who weigh everything carefully before starting, who always check all the details and still find a fly in the ointment in the end, then you should read this point particularly carefully. Everyone knows the phrase If only I ... then ...! If only I had more responsibility, I could achieve more. If I had more power, things would change here. If I had more money, I would be happier.

Such doubts are underhanded. If you think pessimistically, you usually have a distorted perception. Notorious pessimists are no longer able to look at problems from a neutral position from a sufficient distance. Result: You can only see the mountain and no longer the summit. Quite a few then stop in front of the obstacle, turn around, or prefer to take countless, supposedly easier detours. Do not let the conditions chase you down!

You can also reach the summit in stages. Think about where you are and what needs to be done next to get one step closer to that goal. And then go ahead. Stcp by step. Base camp for base camp. If you have never achieved anything, let us go, guys, and achieve everything.

Impatience.

Impatience is a weakness - a big one. I want! Everything! Now! Attitude only creates instant types who desire too fast and too much at once but are not (yet) up to the task (see also overconfidence). You cannot have three years of experience in one. It is the practice that makes perfect.

It takes patience to manage a challenging project and even more so to lead other people. But being able to wait can even be a virtue. Some problems can be solved by themselves, or over time you will receive information and ideas that enable a better solution. The express elevator to a career is and will remain a myth.

There is much more strength in rest. Plus, nothing is more frustrating than climbing the corporate ladder at a rapid pace only to find out at the top that you have laid it on the wrong wall.

Ingratitude

Even geniuses sometimes need the help of others. Be it that they provide you with useful information, warn you in good time, or actively protect you. The more mentors you have, the better. A functioning network of relationships and lots of B vitamins act as a career turbo.

But it can also quickly become a career killer if you forget about your contacts. And it is effortless: Simply forget who was at your side with advice and action and from whom you have benefited in some form so far. No one expects immediate consideration for such favors. Only those who forget this guilt are engaged in self-sabotage of the first order.

Goethe already considered ingratitude to be a weakness: I have never seen capable people being ungrateful. Ingratitude is not a trivial offense but a gross violation of a professional iron law: one hand washes the other.

Aimlessness

That, too, is an iron law of success: strong personalities do not hang around. If you want to give wings to your career, you have to make consistent decisions -

also on your behalf. To do this, however, you first must know exactly what you want. This is the only way to gain clarity in your head and tenacity in action.

Indeed, there are always overly committed people who do not turn down a request and manage several projects simultaneously - but they do not get any further. You have more stress and less fun. If you tackle everything somehow, you do not do anything well. Top performance, on the other hand, only arises when you fully concentrate on a specific goal. Therefore, everyone should (and again and again) ask themselves:

- What exactly do I want to achieve?
- What should change or improve in my life?
- Why is this goal so important to me?
- What must be done to achieve it?
- What can I do?
- Is that enough for that?
- What would I have to do without?

Such goals are welcome to change. After all, clinging to a plan forever or staying too long in a job can also be an expression of aimlessness. The main thing is that you remain aware of it and keep moving. Because it is still like this: a career is not a coincidence - it is made.

As a soon-to-be university grad, I know that the world of work can catch you unaware. In preparing for the job search, I have found that experienced professionals often have great advice to dispense (also some not-so-great advice, but that is a topic for another book).

And, indeed, sometimes the wisest tips do not come from experts but real people with real and true stories. With that in mind, The Muse team requested the LinkedIn community what wisdom they would bestow on recent grads.

More students are eager to work with university certificates, with the yearly competition.

Are you looking for job advice for recent graduates?

If you experience any of these fears:

- You are eager to put your new college degree to use but do not have your perfect job lined up.

- You are worried that you may have a lack of experience.
- You are unsure of what industry you should be in.
- You have never been interviewed and are not sure about preparing.

Career advice for you.

BUSINESS TIPS FOR FRESH COLLEGE GRADUATES

Here are some business tips for recent college graduates that will help you choose a career path that is right for you and land that job out of college that you want.

1. Do Not Let the World Decide Your Path.

Sit down and make a list and a plan of your ideal situation. Ask yourself:

- What type of work do you relish doing?
- If you were not getting paid, what kind of work would you enjoy doing?
- What activities in your past have been responsible for your success?

Making a plan will help put you on the right path to getting a great job.

2. Informational Interviewing

Before an interview, research the company and overall industry you are interviewing for. When you have your consultation, you will be able to tell the interviewer about the industry and ask questions such as: "Where do you foresee this corporation going in the next 3 to 5 years?"

The more questions you ask, the more you control the interview. Do not approach the interview as applying for a job. Consider it as doing an investigation to see if the company or even the industry is right for you. Sometimes you will find that you do not care for either. What you want from a first interview is information.

This information includes:

- Information on what you will be doing.
- Information on the company and company culture.
- Information on the industry and the main industries competitors.

Investigate the Company Fully Before You converse

When you have an interview talk, you must do extensive research on a company. For a one-hour consultation, you should do 3 hours of research into the company.

When you research the company, look at these things:

- Who will be interviewing you?
- The company's website.
- The industry the company is in.
- Does the company have the main competitors? If so, who?
- The products they sell.
- The company's cultures.

Find out as much as you probably can about the group before your interview. You will ask questions about the business, the industry, and the people and get much more out of the initial consultation.

3. Select Your Boss with Care

Make sure that you are convenient with and like your boss. Your boss will influence your pleasure, enjoyment, and success in your career more than anyone else.

4. Request for a little bit More Responsibility

When you finish an assignment at your new job, do not sit on your hands, waiting for someone else to give you a new task. Ask for more responsibility.

What Happens When You Request for More Responsibility?

- Your employer grows to trust that you can do it if there is a job that needs to be done.
- The more duty you ask for, the more you will be rewarded.

Asking for more responsibility will break your career open.

5. Choose Something You Love Over Money

This is a time where you can get to know yourself and find what you love to do. This may be hard to think about in the short run, especially if finding a job is hard.

But think about this, would you instead end up in a career that you hate and earn lots of money or be doing something that you truly love for the rest of your life, earning less money?

6. Visit These Job Sites for Leads on Acquiring A Job in Your Field

There are hundreds of job websites that you can use to look for jobs. I have included a few here:

- LinkedIn
- Indeed
- Simply Hired
- Monster
- Craigslist

7. Your Education Never Ends

Do not worry. This is a good thing. You will always be schooling on new items, reading new books, and developing yourself to be the very best version of yourself. You will be schooled in new facets of a position plus gain expertise plus knowledge. Be open to this change.

8. Use Social Media for Networking

There are many opportunities to network. Social media websites like LinkedIn make it easier than before to get in touch with professionals in your field. Many companies who are hiring scout actively for young professionals individuals on LinkedIn. Certify that you have an updated resume and accomplishment list placed on your profile or your portrait.

Use Facebook to network with your peers from the university. Perhaps they also know a person in an industry you would like to work in.

9. What Microsoft, Hulu, Including Julep Executives Have to Say

---

"The capability to learn quickly and adapt promptly is critical no matter what role you're going in for."

— JULIE GREEN, VP OF DIGITAL
AT JULEP

A panel of tech executives at Western University's

Leadership forum discussed career advice for recent grads.

10. Stay Positive

Always think positively. Remember these two tips when you go for an interview:

- Your interview starts in the parking lot.
- Your examination ends when you leave the building.

Even if you are upset in the interview process, always keep a positive outlook.

Preparation, experience, and a positive perspective will eventually lead you to the perfect job for you.

PLEASE LEAVE A 1-CLICK REVIEW!

I hope you enjoyed reading this book!

If you haven't done so yet, I would be incredibly thankful if you could take 60 seconds to write a brief review on the platform of purchase, even if it's just a few sentences!

Your feedback will be a huge help in helping other readers benefit from the information in the book.

You can also contact us by sending an email to tcecpublishing@outlook.com

Like us on https://www.facebook.com/tcecpublishing/

Join our Facebook page : https://www.facebook.com/groups/800312427190446 to stay updated on our next releases!

See you there!

Your free gift!

Voucher ID: NGH0001

Download your free copy here

https://tcecpublishing.com/tcsf-free-ebook

CONCLUSION

Have you have been in the same position for years as your work colleagues slowly climb the corporate ladder? Do not look for the reason in your environment, but in yourself because most employees stand in their way during career advancement. Take responsibility for yourself, get out there, climb the ladder, and get the career you want. Anything is possible if you use all the tips and advice in this book.

Technical competence is not enough to ensure that your work colleagues do not pass you by. If you want to get ahead, you must show a high level of commitment and continuous development. Always choosing the easiest route is a typical career killer. Taking responsibility for your behaviors and mistakes is not always easy, but it is crucial for your professional future. Sometimes even the little things are enough to have lasting damage to your career. Do not let yourself get stuck in a rut.

A good saying goes, if you love your career, you will never feel like you've worked a day in your life. Do what you love, and do not settle for less!

OTHER BOOKS YOU'LL LOVE!

1. Healthy Habits for Kids: Positive Parenting Tips for Fun Kids Exercises, Healthy Snacks and Improved Kids Nutrition
2. Mini Habits for Happy Kids: Proven Parenting Tips for Positive Discipline and Improving Kids' Behavior
3. Financial Tips to Help Kids: Proven Methods for Teaching Kids Money Management and Financial Responsibility
4. Life Strategies for Teenagers: Positive Parenting Tips and Understanding Teens for Better Communication and a Happy Family
5. 101 Tips for Child Development: Proven Methods for Raising Children and Improving Kids Behavior with Whole Brain Training

6. [101 Tips For Helping With Your Child's Learning: Proven Strategies for Accelerated Learning and Raising Smart Children Using Positive Parenting Skills](#)
7. [Parenting Teen Boys in Today's Challenging World: Proven Methods for Improving Teenagers Behaviour with Whole Brain Training](#)
8. [Parenting Teen Girls in Today's Challenging World: Proven Methods for Improving Teenagers Behaviour with Whole Brain Training](#)
9. [The Fear of The Lord: How God's Honour Guarantees Your Peace](#)
10. [Tips for #CollegeLife: Powerful College Advice for Excelling as a College Freshman](#)
11. [The Motivated Young Adult's Guide to Career Success and Adulthood: Proven Tips for Becoming a Mature Adult, Starting a Rewarding Career, and Finding Life Balance](#)
12. [Career Success Formula Proven Career Development Advice And Finding Rewarding Employment For Young Adults And College Graduates](#)
13. [Developing Yourself as a Teenager](#)
14. [Guide for Boarding School Life](#)

REFERENCES

[1] https://www.psychologytoday.com/us/blog/unified-theory-happiness/201807/7-ways-cope-people-who-want-bring-you-down

[2] https://www.psychologytoday.com/us/blog/living-single/201402/10-steps-getting-over-humiliation

[3] https://workplaceinsight.net/over-three-quarters-of-women-and-more-than-half-of-men-experience-sexism-at-work/

[4] https://workplaceinsight.net/over-three-quarters-of-women-and-more-than-half-of-men-experience-sexism-at-work/

[5] https://www.equalrights.org/issue/economic-workplace-equality/discrimination-at-work/

[6] https://www.equalrights.org/issue/economic-workplace-equality/sexual-harassment/

[7] https://www.lifehack.org/articles/communication/8-benefits-identifying-your-values.html

[8] https://thriveglobal.com/stories/the-power-of-writing-down-your-goals-and-how-to-do-it/

[9] https://www.thebalancecareers.com/tips-choosing-best-job-2060998

[10] https://www.thebalancecareers.com/steps-to-choosing-career-525506

[11] https://www.recruitday.com/blog/fresh-grads-guide-job-hunting

[12] https://guthriejensen.com/blog/tips-to-help-new-graduates-get-employed/

[13] https://www.topresume.com/career-advice/5-tips-to-help-students-prepare-for-their-careers

[14] https://www.topresume.com/career-advice/5-tips-to-help-students-prepare-for-their-careers

[15] https://www.ceu.edu/article/2019-03-29/how-choose-your-thesis-topic

[16] https://www.careeraddict.com/5-benefits-for-students-who-work-part-time-jobs

[17] https://www.quora.com/What-can-a-high-school-student-do-to-prepare-for-their-future-career

[18] https://www.nap.edu/read/19401/chapter/17#429

[19] https://www.allaboutcareers.com/careers-advice/postgraduate-study/professional-qualifications

[20] https://www.jobstreet.com.ph/career-resources/6-reasons-youre-getting-hired#.X51rZ5DivIU

[21] https://www.livecareer.com/questions/2953/what-s-an-unsolicited-cover-letter#:~:text=An%20unsolicited%20cover%20letter%20is%20a%20letter%20that%20expresses%20interest,not%20have%20a%20job%20opening.&text=Since%20you%20are%20writing%20this,inquiry%20to%20a%20specific%20person

[22] https://hk.jobsdb.com/en-hk/articles/10-basic-but-powerful-resume-writing-tips-for-fresh-graduates/

[23] https://www.indeed.com/career-advice/interviewing/job-interview-tips-how-to-make-a-great-impression

[24]   https://www.weforum.org/agenda/2015/06/21-things-you-should-do-on-your-first-day-of-work/

[25]   https://jannalynnhagan.com/blog/2015/8/4/making-a-successful-transition-from-student-to-employee

[26]   https://www.fnu.edu/smooth-transition-student-employee/

[27]   https://social.hays.com/2020/01/29/transition-student-life-to-working-life/

[28]   http://www.inspiringinterns.com/blog/2016/11/how-to-adjust-from-being-a-student-to-an-employee/

www.ingramcontent.com/pod-product-compliance
Lightning Source LLC
Chambersburg PA
CBHW070107120526
44588CB00032B/1375